YOU CHOOSE YOUR LIFE

Same shoes different paths

Marquita D. Dorsey

This page is for copyright info

Marquita Dorsey can be contacted by email at: marquitabookings@gmail.com
marquitadorsey.com

Acknowledgement

I would like to acknowledge my friends for allowing me to tell their stories. They are great women who made choices that changed their lives and they have no regrets. Also, I wanted to thank the 6 girls in my life as they are making choices everyday to be great leaders, sisters, mothers and daughters. My mom and grandmothers for being an inspiration to hard work and resilience. Nevertheless, the inspiration who was always present and never allowed me to give up even in difficult times. "You're the Winner and the One Jesse J "GF"

Marquita D. Dorsey

Note from the inspiration

I applaud your efforts

I see you growing

I got ya back

And I see you winning

I can't wait to read it

It will make the best sellers list

And women all over the world will relate

God bless you with the idea now run with it

You make a book

I make it a movie

I love you and keep up the good work

Table Contents

SAME SHOES DIFFERENT PATHS

Acknowledgement v

Jordan 1

Mia 41

SAME SHOES DIFFERENT PATHS
VOLUME 2

Sydney 61

Brittany 80

Jesse 104

Statistics 119

Please be mindful that this book is written in the mindset of a 15 year old

WORLD WAR JORDAN

Same shoes different paths

Jordan was a tall, brown skinned girl, maybe about 5'11," with very tight eyes and a round face. Her hair was dark brown in color, very thick, and to her shoulder. I was about fourteen years old when I met Jordan. She and I were the same age. We met through her sister, who was one of my closest friends. Jordan was really cool, but would never say too much; however, although she was very quiet, she had a slick tongue. Jordan and her sister always had on the freshest gym shoes with a matching vest, which was the style we all were rocking at that time. Since her sister and I were together daily, she was always with us.

Jordan and I quickly became friends after her sister left to go be with her boyfriend in Minnesota. Shameka was pregnant, and for several weeks she had been planning to go and live with her baby's father, who had recently moved to Minnesota. One weekend, Shameka told their mother that she was out of town with me and my mother on a shopping trip, when she was really headed to Minnesota to be with her soon to be baby's father. Many of the young men from our area, the "Low End," went there to sell drugs in order to get more bang for their buck. Shameka's baby's father was like all the young boys our age who were trying to make a name for themselves in the streets, and the only way they knew how was to make more money than the next man, or have enough courage to shoot if the need presented itself.

Shameka was determined to see her child's father despite her mother's disapproval of him. Jordan knew her sister's plan to chase this boy nine hours away in another state. Shameka's baby's father called her to let her know that he had sent her money through Western

Union, which she picked up and proceeded to the Greyhound station where he had her ticket waiting at the counter. Shameka was well on her way before her mother finally caught on that she was not at home. When she had not heard from Shameka, she was livid.

Jordan and Shameka's mom was hardcore and she didn't bite her tongue for no one. She let it be known what was on her mind despite how anyone felt about what she was saying. She didn't like many people, especially most of her daughters' friends who she either thought were phony or full of shit and she had no problem telling them that when they were around. When she realized that Shameka was gone, she hit the roof shouting obscenities about her daughter's whereabouts, yelling about whether she thought that she was grown. Jordan called me to give me the heads up about her mother's outrage, so I knew to stay away. Shameka called us when she made it to Minnesota, and she told us about all the things that she was doing while she was there. However, once she talked to her mother, Shameka had come up with an outrageous lie that she was on a shopping trip with me and my mother. Her mother did not care who she was with. She told Shameka that she was not grown, and that she would deal with her as soon as she got "her raggedy ass" home, so she needed to shorten the trip or she would call the "god damn" police because she was underage and should not be out without her permission. Shameka really thought this lie through because she was aware that her mother didn't know where I lived. Her mom knew who I was, so I had to stay away from Jordan and their home while Shameka was on her rendezvous in Minnesota. I ended up staying away from their home for a few weeks because their mom was rough, and she would cuss anyone out and I was no different. When Shameka returned home, safe and sound, I decided to stay away because her mother did not really like me, and I did not want to get caught up in the drama.

Jordan was really upset that Shameka had lied and got her caught up in her drama, especially because she had her own issues that she was keeping a secret. However, Jordan was really upset with her sister and she was beginning to feel overwhelmed. Shameka seemed to get away with so much and Jordan knew that if she had pulled the same stunt her mother would kill her, possibly kick her out, or possibly call the police.

Since Shameka had forced me and her sister to lie for her, Jordan and I had to speak to each other continuously to ensure we were capable of keeping up with the lies she was telling. She couldn't understand why her sister would tell such an outrageous lie. The constant calling between Jordan and I was the beginning of a never-ending friendship, which we still have today. We were inseparable after this incident, and the friendship that I originally had with Shameka began to decline because I Jordan and I started speaking with each other more than before.

Soon after our friendship blossomed, Jordan had a baby. She had lost her virginity months before her sister had gotten pregnant. No one knew Jordan was pregnant as she hid it from everybody. She had given her innocence to a guy who was older than us named Emmanuel, who was a drug dealer. She was fourteen at the time. He wasn't that attractive, but she wanted him and that's all that mattered to her. He was dark skinned, with a big head. He wasn't that tall, but he was a nice height. He was one of those young men who stood on the corner after school and menaced society. He wasn't a person that a mother would want her daughter to date, but he was all that she knew. He dressed in the latest gear which at this time were Coogi and Iceberg. He was always fresh and that was one of the things Jordan admired about him. There were several girls who flocked to him, however at that time Jordan was determined to be his girlfriend and she beat out the competition. There weren't many boys to choose from so the hood boys were all the girls had.

When you think you are in love you do a lot of things not realizing until much later in life that it wasn't love at all. Jordan was never one to give up and I think that's why she loved him. The challenge he gave her made her proud to be with him. Every good girl needed a bad boy, at least that was the frame of mind she had at the time. She thought that Emmanuel loved her, so she gave in to him. At the time she thought this was the appropriate thing to do. She was really too young to know what real love was, but she felt that she was in love with Emmanuel. The first time they had sex was in an abandoned apartment in the 1st building, which was a building in the housing projects known as Newtown. These apartments were furnished with beds and couches. All the boys brought their girlfriends to these apartments and there were at least two empty apartments in each building. Occasionally we would hang out in those empty apartments.

Jordan's first sexual encounter with Emmanuel was painful. She described the pain as excruciating, but she laid there trying to hold the tears back. He broke her hymen but didn't get much closer to entering her than that. His penis was too large to enter her vagina, and she had to let him know that it hurt too bad. After noticing that this was an uncomfortable situation for her, he decided not to go further with the process. Days after the act her vagina still ached and it was still swollen. She couldn't tell her mother of the pain because she didn't want her to know that she had tried to have sex. She kept the pain to herself and hoped that it would go away. Many days after her attempt at her first sexual encounter she found out that her boyfriend had been with other girls. In disgust, she no longer wanted to talk to him.

Several months after dating Emmanuel, Jordan met a young man named Brett. Everyone knew she was upset about her recent breakup with Emmanuel, but Brett came along and swept her off her feet. He was a tall brown skinned young man with a long head and round eyes. He wasn't a hood boy and he actually seemed kind of lame. He danced his way into her heart. She was really into him because of his membership in a dance group called Phase 2. Phase 2 was one of the top dance groups in Chicago and he was a skilled dancer, so she liked that about him. He was different from her last boyfriend, which I thought was a good thing. His mother was very involved in his life and Jordan met her on several different occasions. Since no one had let her meet their mother before this made her feel important, and she liked Brett even more. Brett was definitely different that the boys she was used to, at least that was the persona he was giving everyone.

It wasn't long after she went to a few of his practices that they were together as boyfriend and girlfriend. Before long, he too wanted her to give in to his mannish thoughts, and she complied. Now this experience was just as painful as the first. Not once did they ask one another about protection. He tried for what seemed like hours to enter her. Although she cried, he still couldn't get himself to stop. He wanted what he came there for, her body. He told her to just lay there and take the pain and she did, laying there stiff as a board never moving except only to wipe her tears. At last he entered her. Although her vagina was throbbing, he continued to pounce in and out of it. She didn't say a word. She couldn't wait for it to be over and at last it was. He let out a moan that she hadn't heard before, then laid on top of her. She didn't know what was happening as this was all new to her. She asked if he was ok, and he told her he had ejaculated. She didn't know what he meant, so she continued to lay still. Once she returned home, she felt something running down her leg, and that's when she knew what ejaculation. During her first real sexual experience, she became pregnant. She didn't know she was pregnant right away and by the time she got the first hint, it was too late for her to choose other options like abortion. She never told anyone she was pregnant, and I don't think anyone noticed. She was in love and no one could tell her any different.

A few weeks after her first encounter with Brett, Jordan began to feel different. She was nauseous and was sleeping more than usual. Although she was throwing up every day all day, everyone thought she was sick with a stomach virus. She barely woke up to attend school, so when her mother made her go, she just went over to Brett's house because his mother was working when they were supposed to be in school. Shortly after her first trimester she felt better, but then she was trying to hide her stomach which was growing at a rapid speed. She had lost weight before she started to gain weight. This helped her hide her pregnancy better and she succeeded a whole nine months.

Two weeks before she gave birth, she received a phone call from her aunt stating that she knew she was pregnant. Jordan was upset and her first reaction was to lie to her aunt. She knew her cousin told on her and she wasn't going to have anyone judge her, so her defenses were up. Her cousin, who was the same age as she, had just had a baby and told on her so that everyone could know she wasn't the only one having sex at a young age. After she calmed down, Jordan admitted to her aunt that she was pregnant. She knew it wasn't long before everyone would know anyway. Her aunt offered to call her mother and give her the news and Jordan agreed only if her aunt didn't tell her mother while she was at work. Before she could hang up the phone, the phone rang again with her mother asking if the rumors were true. Jordan confirmed to her that they were. Her mother was upset and told her she would speak to her when she returned home from work.

Once her mother got home they talked about her plans for the future. Her mother explained to her that having a child is the hardest task in the world. She let Jordan know that she made her life ten times harder and assured her that she would help her with anything she needed but that she would be responsible for her own child. Jordan cried, her mother consoling her, but she knew her mother meant every word that she said. Jordan had some growing up to do and fast. After the talk she made her a doctor's appointment, the doctor told her that he wanted to schedule an ultrasound. When she went for the ultrasound, she was running a fever and the doctor decided to induce labor. Jordan cried uncontrollably on her way to the hospital thinking that she would be someone's mother once she returned home. Reality had finally set in and she was scared. She knew there would be no more "I" it would be "we".

The doctor contacted her mother, and she came to the hospital. Jordan was in labor for nineteen hours because her water bag wouldn't burst. By her being so young she hadn't developed all the way so the doctors didn't want to harm her or the baby. Finally, the doctors decided to burst her water bag and she went on to deliver a beautiful baby boy. Brett's mother was at the hospital too. They didn't say too much, but once they saw the baby they couldn't stop talking about how cute and adorable he was. These gestures made Jordan think that everything was going to work out for the best between her and the child's father. She hoped that one day they could be together as a family. Two days later Jordan left the hospital with her healthy baby boy.

Fifteen and a mother still hadn't stuck into her head once she returned home. Jordan had gotten away with hiding a pregnancy like many young girls do when they find themselves in that position. Never once did she grasp the fact that maybe the secret would harm her child. All expectant mothers need medical care. She was too young and immature to know what she was doing or what her actions had done to the people around her. Not every young girl is as blessed as Jordan to have a healthy child after nine months of pregnancy with no medical care. Jordan's mother had another mouth to feed and clothed. She put more strain on her mother.

Same shoes different paths

After the birth of her son, we were inseparable. I can remember working, and on various occasions she would call and ask if I could purchase her son's milk and pampers. Without any hesitations I did any and everything for her, never asking for anything in return. As the friendship I had with Jordan grew stronger, my friendship with Shameka drifted apart, although we were always going to be friends no matter what happened.

Her son's father was never really involved in his life besides being at the hospital. One day he was around and the next day he wasn't. He was playing games with the relationship he was supposed to be having with his son's relationship. He did come and get the baby a few times but it was like he really wasn't feeling the situation. His mother wasn't even interacting with her grand-child. She didn't even make her son take responsibility for the child he helped create. As she began to move on with her life, Brett stopped claiming the baby as his son. After feeling the rejection from her son's father, she went back with Emmanuel. Emmanuel argued with her about her having a baby, while deep down inside he wanted her son to be his. He was actually telling everyone that the baby looked like him. Although Jordan told him that the baby was not his, he refused to believe it, and still believes it to this day. He stopped arguing the issue and let Jordan be. Emmanuel and Jordan had sexual intercourse one more time and they ended up parting ways. Emmanuel starting dating someone else. Shortly after hearing about the incident with Emmanuel, she learned that Brett, her child's father, ended up having a baby with someone she had known all her life. Even though she and this other girl weren't friends they did know one another. This hurt her, but she couldn't let in kill her spirit.

In the summer of 2000, Jordan began to date a new guy named Lamont. Lamont was dark skinned, average height, with a huge stomach. Lamont was a jean and white tee shirt, with gym shoes kind of guy. Very loud and disrespectful, he didn't even respect his mother. Every other word out of his mouth was "bitch," or "whore." You couldn't even have a typical conversation with him. He was the type of man that woke up drinking and went to sleep drinking. Jordan knew Lamont for a while and I really can't explain how they began dating. I really didn't object to her dating this guy, but I knew of his violent background. Everyone knows everyone in the projects. Lamont was known for beating up his girlfriends. I'm talking breaking arms, black eyes, and busted lips. I can remember the first time Lamont and Jordan had a fight. It was under one of the buildings in Madden Park Homes (Newtown). I can't remember why they were fighting, but I was there with her. After the fight began to go too far and he started swinging and pulling her hair, I decided I was no longer going to watch so I tried to help. On this particular day Jordan's mother was looking for her. After the fight she went home. Jordan decided to still be with this man after fighting with him, so I vowed to never interfere with their issues again. Once Jordan returned home, her mother went off because she knew Jordan had been fighting with Lamont. Jordan's mother let her know that she did not like what was happening. Her mother told her that she was stupid to want to continue being bothered with this man. Although she knew her mother didn't approve of the relationship, she continued to do what she wanted when she wanted.

By the time Jordan had her son, then started to be with Lamont, she had stopped going to school and to this day I can't understand why. She was really making horrible decisions, but we all were at this time in our lives. She even started spending nights out and not coming home for days. Her actions caused her mother not to like Lamont even more. He never really encouraged her to finish school so she just gave up on furthering her education. He didn't want her to do anything without him and she had no problem living with those restrictions.

The year of my high school graduation, things in Jordan's life began to spiral downwards. Jordan was raised by her mother and step father who came along shortly after her sister was born. Her biological father couldn't deny her if he wanted because she looked just like him. Her father, like the father of her eldest son was never really involved in her life. I can remember him promising her things and never coming through with them. This made her upset but she continued to move on with her life despite the pain or loneliness she felt from him not being around. I believed she wanted her father around and she missed him telling her that she was beautiful and that he loved her. At different times in our lives, as young ladies, we miss out on different ingredients that complement our souls and help make us better women. She never really did speak to him often and she liked it that way.

The relationship she was in with Lamont started getting very serious. Making continuous bad decisions led her to a second pregnancy. I didn't even know she was expecting, until one day Jordan called me crying stating that, she and "Lamont had a fight the previous night and her side was hurting badly." Lamont had kicked her in the stomach and even busted her lip. Once I learned of the seriousness of the fight, I went to meet her and we went to the nearest emergency room. We found out after her examination that she was having a miscarriage. She didn't tell anyone of this incident, and I understood she was hurting emotionally so I just continued to console her.

    I thought that after the miscarriage this abusive relationship was over for sure. Just the opposite happened, the relationship had gotten even more serious. Right after the miscarriage she found out she was pregnant again. She ended up having another baby boy who was equally as gorgeous as her first son. After the birth of the second child, Jordan continued to lose herself. She still was not going home, and she spent all her time with Lamont. He didn't have his own residence, so they stayed over his friend's house where everyone hung out. They never had any privacy at this house because there was always several people there, or in and out all times of the night. Jordan knew this wasn't the best environment for her and the kids, but she continued to be there because it made him happy. The turning point soon came when she arrived at this house and there was another girl there. Jordan knew the girl, but she wasn't expecting to see her up close and personal. This girl was a constant disturbance in Jordan and Lamont's relationship. The young lady claimed that she and Lamont were also dating and he was the father of her child. She tried to ignore this situation but in the projects these types of incidents can't be ignored. This young lady came around often and he seemed to not to be able to make her leave. Jordan continued to see this girl and the situation made her feel uncomfortable, so she stopped going to this house because she didn't want the situation escalating. Her mother was glad to see her coming home more. This did not change how Jordan felt about Lamont. Despite all of what had happened, she was still in love with him.

Same shoes different paths

Soon after the summer was over the city decided to demolish all the city of Chicago's projects. Jordan and I hated the idea of no longer being able to hang out and enjoy ourselves. One day the housing project closed, and she no longer lived in Ida B. Wells. Jordan, her mother, her two siblings, her two children, and her nephew moved to the Englewood neighborhood. She didn't really want to change her environment, but she had no choice. While living there with her mother, she continued to date Lamont. She didn't see him that much which gave him the opportunity to see other young ladies. After a short period of time she was able to receive living assistance from the city so she no longer would be living with her mother. She moved into her own place with her children and of course her man. Jordan and her children loved their new place. She thought because the projects no longer existed, they were going to have a great relationship. It wasn't long before he continued to be misleading and devious. He was beginning to come home late. Sometimes he wouldn't answer when she called him. Even when he decided to come home, his phone would ring all times of the night. Sometimes he would answer and other times he wouldn't answer. When he did answer, females would be on the other end of the phone. Once again she found herself not knowing what to do regarding his infidelity. She continued to disregard his actions as his behavior wouldn't change.

Only a month after living in her new apartment Jordan found out she was pregnant. She couldn't believe this situation had presented itself once again, plus this time she was taking birth control. She felt as if the walls were closing in on her life fast. How could she admit to anyone, especially her mother, who was helping her with the children financially, that she was pregnant again? She knew her mother wouldn't like the fact that she continued to have kids without furthering her education or even having a job. Like many young girls, she was back again facing a hard reality of deciding whether to raise, to abort or give up the child for adoption. She battled with her beliefs and the best decision for her other children. She ended her battle with deciding against abortion and adoption.

After dealing with her personal struggles, she told her man that she was pregnant. I really don't think she wanted to tell him, but she had no choice. She knew he would find out sooner or later. He had about two other kids besides the one she had with him, and the one on the way that she was pregnant with. Upon finishing their conversation, he told her that things would get better and that he would change. To prove this to her he went out and bought her a ring. She thought that this was the greatest thing ever. He proposed, he asked for her hand in marriage and she happily accepted. This was to be a new beginning, but it soon came to a crashing end fast. He couldn't change or let's just say, he wouldn't change. A while later she knew he had no intentions on changing, he just wanted to pacify her so that she would not complain. He had excelled in his mission to calm her but not for long.

Jordan had a baby shower about a month before she was due. She had just turned twenty one and was getting ready to have her third child. She went into the hospital on her due date, and hours later had a baby girl. The baby was as cute as can be and looked just like her father. After returning home she could feel the struggle getting harder. Don't get me wrong, Lamont did contribute to the household. He loved all three of the kids and did treat her oldest like his own child. This was one reason why I believe she kept him around. On the other hand, I can remember days after she came home from the hospital and she was home cleaning and walking the kids to school. Now she never let things like this break her, but he was at home when she was doing these things. She was going to the laundromat on her own, lugging bags and the kids. She wasn't supposed to be a single parent, but although she was living someone, that is exactly what she was. She continued to play down situations like these and would put on the independent act when things would happen. He didn't even acknowledge the fact that she was struggling with the kids, or even take them out as a family. He continued to run the streets and not take care of home.

Jordan had to take her children everywhere she went; no one would watch the kids for her. She continued to walk everywhere or get on the bus for doctor appointments with her baby on her hip and the other kids walking behind her. Every moment of every day, she got a full understanding of what it was like to be a single mother. She learned that although she was with someone, who would sometimes show their face and purchasing a few things, it didn't mean that they were there because they loved you or for the benefit of the children. Her heart was turning cold, yet she continued to yearn for support, respect and true love. I tried to be the best friend I could be and support her in any way I could. Having this third child didn't make anything easier or better for her. She still couldn't find a job although she wanted one. She couldn't afford daycare or a way to get back and forward if she did get a job. So she continued to make ends meet by getting assistance from the state to help support her children. She understood that in certain cases the system didn't assist you, it handicapped you. She told me several times about how she could be doing so much better with her life. By this time she still hadn't received a high school diploma or GED, She knew she needed to finish. She still hadn't worked besides a summer job. She continued to ask herself how she was going to get things better in her and the children lives.

Just when she thought things in her life couldn't get more complicated, they did. Her boyfriend had started to be home a lot more and she thought maybe things were finally changing for the better. She soon realized that her dream or hope for happiness was not going to happen, when one day she received a knock on the door, and it was the police. She opened the door, they asked for her children's father as they proceeded to enter, and they took her boyfriend into custody. She didn't understand what was going on, so she called his family and told them what happened. After finding out where his bond hearing was, she went to be there for his support. At the hearing is where her world took a turn; the state had charged her man with first degree murder and bond was denied. She just cried while gathering her daughter's belongings, leaving the courtroom with her head hung down low. She couldn't believe that this was happening to her and she had no doubt in her mind that this was all untrue. Her hope for a happy life with Lamont, was not going to happen. She knew there wasn't any coming back from this unless the judge was willing to give him bond. Her man had to sit in jail for what was going to be a long time.

Every visiting day she had to visit him. She even took the kids along with her, sometimes waiting until they were in school. She tried her best to be supportive of Lamont and his situation. He would call her several times a week and she made sure she was at home for every call. She probably had three different house phone carriers during his first year of his incarceration. She would change providers when her bill grew too rapidly. He would have his friends or family members stop by and drop off a little money when he was in desperate need for the funds. However, people giving you something in your time of need doesn't last long. After a while she just stopped asking or accepting money from people. Lamont had damn near exhausted his funds on the streets soon after his arrival at the county jail.

For months she went to the county faithfully, but after seeing that this wasn't changing his outlook on life, she didn't go as much. To add salt to the wound, there were several occasions when she would visit Lamont and there would be other women there waiting to see him. This was beginning to be a never-ending story for her. One minute they were together and next she was receiving letters saying that she wasn't worthy of him. He would call and argue about things that happened in the past or things that he heard. I can remember one time he called her and asked when she was going to get a job. He wanted her to get the job so that she could send him some money because he felt like she wasn't contributing to his books or lawyer fees. He never asked her to get the job so that she can have a better chance supporting the kids while he was locked up. She didn't put him there, but he made her feel guilty about him being there. Jordan went back and forward with these childish antics. She just thought that him trying to manipulate her was the right thing for him to be doing. She knew he was hurting so she took the hollering, cussing, and disrespect. When her feelings were hurt, she would change her number and wouldn't give it to him as punishment. This punishment went on for a couple of days and then they were back in love. The phone number changing happened on several occasions. I guess you go through things until you're tired and no one has to make that decision but you.

After about a year of being broken, she decided to pick herself up and put the pieces back together. She gave Lamont a rest and dusted herself off. She even became a more involved parent. She still took the kids to see their father every week, but she made sure it didn't interfere with their education. A change was coming over Jordan and she couldn't help but to gloat about it. She let everyone know that she was not allowing anyone to rain on her parade or cause stress in her life. Believe me, everyone was not happy about this sudden change, and even worried about where this change was coming from. About a year and a half later Jordan decided to move from her current residence. One evening when she wasn't at home someone kicked in her door and stole some items. This scared her and she didn't know what to do, she replaced the locks on the door. Without a man around she no longer felt safe in the home alone and she decided to stay with her mother. That's when she began to inquire about a new place. Once she found a new home. She and the children moved. What a great new start!

I don't think Jordan realized what great responsibilities she took on for herself once she moved into her new place. A month after living in her new apartment the gas bill came and it was far more than what she expected. She was aware that it was her responsibility to pay for utilities and gas. This decision to move in a new place and not really realizing the burden she was going to have made her feel bad. She became tired of asking people for money to help her get out of a tight hole. So she vowed to find a new job and after about three months she did. I was so proud of her and I let her know how excited I was for her.

Through this process of her making positive changes that took her almost three years to complete, Jordan had been through countless hearings and court dates. Every time she got the free time to be in court to show her support of Lamont, she went. It seemed as if this case was going to go on forever, a never-ending saga. Over two years, the children are getting older and missing their father, and no change in sight. He continued to let her know he would rather be home with her and the kids. Jordan always seemed to believe in him despite the past and present situations. One day he called and told her that his trial was going to begin. She was stunned she didn't know what she was going to do. She was excited and fearful at the same time. Her excitement stemmed from her hope that he would be home soon, while she feared that he would never come home. Once the trial started, he was in court almost every other day. The times she was able to make it, she was sure to be there, but when she had to work, she could not attend. She really hoped he understood. The judge told them in the courtroom that once she made the decision both families would be pleased with the verdict. This made everyone gasp for air not knowing what the verdict would be. Jordan called me the day before the trial would conclude and asked if I would pray for her and him. I prayed for God to ensure that the right decision was made, and to give her strength no matter what the decision. The beginning of the end or the end of the beginning came, and the judge found him...Not guilty of First-Degree Murder!

She really didn't know whether to feel excited or upset. She called me and told me the news, and then she went to work. She had not been with this man in three years. She continued to ask herself about how he was going to be. Not really knowing if things were going to be good, she allowed herself to be excited. She was really afraid because she had changed so much. She wasn't the same naive young lady she was before. How was he going to react to her new found attitude and personality? She knew that if he came home not learning anything from this experience that this would be the end for them.

When he got home, she and the kids were both excited. He spent quality time with them the first night and went to bed early. Pretty soon, after returning home he began being outside more than he was at home. Jordan didn't say anything about him not being home initially. She started feeling like she had made a fool of herself. She let him move in and it felt like before he went to jail. After being home about a week he told Jordan that they were going to city hall and make it official. She went back and forth in her mind, contemplating if getting married was the right thing for her to do. Later in the evening she told him that she would be honored to be his wife. He explained to her that he would have to cheat on her a couple of times before they stood in front of a judge. She was devastated. Her head began to spin. She couldn't believe that he had betrayed her once again. How could he even fix his mouth to say these things? She had to realize and accept that he had not changed. She let him know that she was no longer interested in marriage, and that marriage wasn't for them.

Jordan didn't make him leave even after this incident. I guess she was holding on to what she thought could make her happy, while, she was unhappy. He continued to disregard her feelings, treating her as if she was a doormat for him to walk. They would argue about him not being home or him not spending time with the kids. He had only been out for about a month and she had already grown tired of his antics. He called her and let her know he was going to another woman's house, plus had other women calling his phone. Jordan knew some of these women because she had run ins with them before. They knew he was living with her and they just didn't care. One night, he decided that he was not going home; by the next morning all his bags were packed and waiting by the door. She called and told him she no longer wanted to be involved with him and only wanted him to have a relationship with the kids. She told him to come and get all of his things or she would sit them outside. He threatened to harm her physically if she didn't get her attitude in order. She advised him that if he tried to harm her in any way, she would call the police and send him back to jail. He knew that she meant every word that she said.

The night after she told her man not to return to her home she went to her mothers. She never explained to her mother why she was there but her mother assumed that it was her children's father. That night ended shortly because just when she went to lay down her phone and mothers bell began to ring. It was Lamont. He was drunk and crying, apologizing for his actions. She said she wouldn't listen to him begging, but of course she did. After his apologizing and begging, she went back home with Lamont. Jordan tried to stick with her plan of not dealing with this man and he made it hard for her. She could not resist him when he started crying. Although she tried, they agreed that they would work things out once again.

It wasn't long after getting back together that they were on the outs again. This time she didn't ask him to leave, she just decided that she would go on with her life whether he left or not. He was back doing the same things as usual. There was one incident where his phone was ringing while he was asleep. She answered and it was a woman on the other end of the phone. The woman hung up and instead of calling the number back she read the messages. One message said that she had a great time with him the other night, she missed and loved him. After confronting him he told her he took this woman to a hotel but they didn't do anything but talk. Now what woman in her right mind believes something like that? While she did not show her anger, she was boiling on the inside; but he immediately was again in tears apologizing. The next step for his award-winning performance was trying to make her have sex with him, thinking it would make her feel better. She refused the sex and he forced himself on her by choking her until she gave in to his sexual desire. His actions were becoming worse, more women were calling him, and she just laid back and took these antics, not asking him to leave. Once, he made a statement to her that he needed these other women so that he could manipulate them into doing things she didn't want to do. Sounds crazy, but he had no problem with telling it to her.

Just when I thought I could not write any more about Jordan's story, more tragedy hit her and the children. There was a young lady that she heard Lamont was seeing on the side. Her name was Lisa. He had apparently been seeing Lisa since the day he got out of jail. Now Lisa knew about his relationship with Jordan but didn't care. She had made up her mind to get with Lamont by any means. After Jordan received several calls regarding this, she confronted him and of course he denied the accusations. She was being made into a fool because she he knew that he was always lying to her. After searching through his phone and reading his text messages, she knew he was sleeping with Lisa. Lisa was in love with Lamont, and she was making it known. Their relationship had to have gotten deep if they were talking love. While the texts she saw were only coming from Lisa, as Lamont had erased all the messages he was sending her, Jordan felt that she had enough proof to support her claims of cheating and she confronted him with her findings. Several attempts later, she finally got some answers. More lies, but she still let him stay.

Lamont thought that because Jordan no longer asked about Lisa like she forgot that his extra relationship didn't exist. Immediately after the fire was starting to lose its flare someone threw gas on the cinders to ignite it again. Jordan received a few phone calls regarding Lamont having a baby on the way by Lisa. Jordan's mind-set was trampled. She thought that despite her progress, her personal relationship always resulted in chaos. She confronted him after a while of trying to find the correct words to say. She asked why he didn't tell her that Lisa was pregnant by him. He let her know that he only had sex with Lisa a few times so it couldn't be his baby.

I guess as you are reading this, you're as outraged as I am. I couldn't believe that he thought she would believe that. He told her that Lisa also had a boyfriend so more than likely it was her boyfriend's child. That didn't matter to Jordan, she just wanted Lamont to understand that it only takes one sexual encounter for him to make a child so the excuse he was giving her was simply garbage. Jordan tried to not let these ongoing issues bother her, but they did. It seemed that no issue went without discussion amongst other people when it came to Lamont. She had to realize that because Lamont never went outside of the circle of people they both knew, it was easy for people to talk, and she heard everything. These girls were always someone she knew or knew of and that's why it made their situation so difficult to work out. She couldn't deal with his demeanor about all the things that had been going on since he had come home and then he had the nerve to act as if everything was her fault. They continued to argue and bicker about the past and the present and once again Jordan had asked him to leave her home. As usual he would leave and return, or his friends would call and tell her he was crying wanting her to forgive him. Sometimes he would even be passed out drunk and they would call her to help him in the house. Knowing he had nowhere to go, she felt sorry for him. She did not want to deny him a place to stay and lay his head.

Misfortune was always very close, striking just when she felt that everything was working out for the better. After two months of irregular periods, Jordan got bad news. After the second month she went to the doctor and learned that she was two and a half months pregnant. Her heart fell to the floor. What was she going to do with another baby? She went home and cried because that world of chaos that she worked so hard to get away from had come back and the load was twice as heavy. When no one was around, she cried until she fell asleep. Her actions were once again landing her into a deeper hole. Jordan decided to tell Lamont about the pregnancy. She called him and told him to come home so that they could talk and hours later he came home. Lamont came home drunk, so he said nothing at all.

Lamont's behavior had not changed. When I spoke with her about the new baby, she let me know that she was not keeping it. She was tired of Lamont's behavior and was not going to allow herself to be knocked down any longer, a new baby was going to cause her situation to be worse. She was becoming fed up with his nonchalant attitude and constant cheating and lack of interest he had with her and the children. It was time for him to get out of her home and she knew this time was coming. The day had come and she was at home contemplating back and forward about how she was going to get him to leave this time. She had spoken with her landlord about having her locks changed. In the end, Jordan decided not to get the locks changed as she felt that they were going to fight their way through these hard times.

I was finished with Jordan once again when I got word that Lamont was shot on the fourth of July while watching fireworks. He was shot once in the back and once in the thigh. Jordan got the phone call at about two in the morning that they were rushing him to the hospital. She jumped up and made a few phone calls and found out he was at Cook County Hospital listed in critical condition. Once she arrived at the hospital, she found several of his friends, family members, and alleged exes at the hospital. Before she could find out about how he was doing she hit the roof. She wanted to know why and how his friends and family could have those women at the ER. Why would they have them there discussing her fiancé and what had happened? She felt totally disrespected. After getting almost everyone to leave the ER she found that Lamont was stable but had to be resuscitated a few times and would require surgery.

After a few days Lamont began to progress in health and gain consciousness. Being there all the time caused Jordan to notice that he was going in and out of consciousness. She would be speaking to him and he would nod off. Once he was awake, he wouldn't remember the conversation they had just minutes before. This made Jordan very concerned, but she never allowed him to see her worrying. She was spending more time at the hospital with Lamont, and less time with the children hoping it would bring their family closer. As time passed, things began to look better for Lamont and his health. Jordan was praying for Lamont to be better. She had even started to plan to be his caregiver once he was fit to go home after his rehab. Her life was going to change and with no doubt in her mind, she was willing to give him her all. While she was planning for this, I received a phone call two days later stating that Lamont had turned for the worse. Lamont wasn't looking up and his health was failing fast. Jordan was devastated as she just couldn't handle the news that she had gotten. She rushed to the hospital and she found Lamont to be unresponsive. He wasn't breathing on his own and he did look the same. Jordan was pacing the room not knowing what to say or what to do. She fell on her knees and began to ask GOD to think of their children. She cried and cried but after two days of praying and hoping for his recovery she was called by his sister to meet with the family at the hospital. She arrived at the hospital, greeted by his family and the doctors told them the horrible news. Lamont wasn't going to make it. The doctors told them that they spent the night resuscitating and trying to stabilize him, but that there was nothing more they could do. Jordan went in the room and began to cry telling Lamont to fight for his life and his heart stopped. The doctors ran in and tried to resuscitate him, but she soon realized that Lamont had given up and was no longer with her. She cried and shortly after his grandmother made the decision to take him off the support and he was pronounced dead. Jordan had gathered her thoughts because her mind was racing. Then she felt a sense of calmness over her and knew her day was just getting started.

Once she was leaving the hospital she began to cry wondering how she would break the news, and what she was going to tell her children. She knew that telling them would be the part that destroyed her. She avoided the children once she arrived to her mother's home because looking at them reminded her of Lamont and it made her sad. She forced herself not to tell them that day. Later that evening someone slipped and said something regarding Lamont's death and her oldest child overheard what was said. He asked his mother if what he heard was true, and she had to fight back the tears as she told him what happened. As the tears welled up in his eyes, she could feel the sorrow from his heart reach hers. She held him close to her and assured him that it would be ok. She held him until he fell asleep in her arms. Jordan loved her children and she wanted nothing more than for her kids to be happy. That night, she prayed for peace of mind and a new beginning. The next morning, she awoke feeling a little relief come over her and she felt as if her prayer had been answered. She spoke with her children and they cried together but never once thinking of the bad times only focusing on the good.

It was a couple of days after Lamont's death and her phone was ringing off the hook. Everyone was calling to get the latest on funeral arrangements and finally the decision was made. The Funeral would be exactly eleven days after he had departed from the earth. Jordan was running around trying to find things for her children to wear while trying to get herself together emotionally. The days were going by fast and she was even writing a passage in the obituary. She had a lot going on and she was trying her best to keep her composure, especially in front of the children. As the days passed, she just continued to pray for strength.

The day of the funeral arrived, and Jordan couldn't seem to get organized. She thought of not going to the funeral because she had several people tell her and show her pictures of Lamont in his casket. Jordan was beginning to second guess herself. She felt that she probably did not need to go to the funeral. It was a few hours before the limo was scheduled to pick her and the children up and she finally decided that she would attend. She began to get herself and the children ready and then it was time for them to leave. The bell rang and the children ran to the door. It was their other grandmother and the limo outside. Walking to the limo, Jordan began to cry. She smiled as we waved to her. Once I arrived at the funeral Jordan sat in the front of the service with her head held high never once worrying what others might say. Lamont's family really tried to show appreciation to Jordan at the service. They let her know that she did all that they were unable to do for Lamont. Jordan cried when they gave this special tribute to her and the children. She felt joy and love once the funeral was over. She thanked the family and vowed to be the best mother that she could be from that moment on.

She prayed again that night and thanked GOD for the strength he had given her to make it through the day. She lay to sleep that night thinking about how and what she would do to make her life much more meaningful. The tears ran from her eyes like water as she felt the puddle in the bed where he used to sleep. Smelling his pillow, she finally closed her eyes and went to sleep in peace. Jordan has a long fight ahead of her especially with a new baby. At the age of twenty-six Jordan will be a single mother of four. She decided against abortion after the death of Lamont. The baby will be born exactly six months after his death. She continues to work while raising her children hoping every day that the next will be easier.

Jordan is working and can turn her job into a career with a little more education. She continues to be a single parent raise her children to the best of her abilities. Her oldest son's father still hasn't had any contact with him and he's now nine years old. Jordan hopes that maybe all the drama in her life will end because she's becoming a new person. She's taking her life one day at a time and praying that she continues to make better decisions in her life. She advises all young women to stay strong and know that they deserve better.

CIVIL
WAR
MIA

I was ten, in the fifth grade, when I met Mia. She was a new student to my fifth-grade class; a tall, dark-skinned, skinny girl with slender facial features and a gap in her two front teeth. When we met, she was wearing her hair in a jheri curl and soon, she blew her hair dry and got braces on her teeth. We became friends in no time because she was very nice and had a quiet nature. There was a group of five young girls who would hang out together, but Mia, myself and another girl would be together all the time. We spent most of our days in class having a good time, and by night we were always on the phone talking about the good times we had during the day.

Mia had a younger sister and younger brother who also attended our school. We were always wondering why she refused to take us to her house. She told us she lived in South Commons which was like an upscale apartment complex, but truly, she resided in Prairie Commons (PCs) which was a Chicago housing project. I never understood why she lied to us, but we got past it. Shortly after we found out, her family ended up moving to a four-bedroom, two-bathroom grey stone. They moved in with her aunt, uncle and their two girls. Her two cousins were of the same age as Mia and her sister. Mia, her sister and her mother shared a room and her brother had his own bedroom to himself. Interestingly, everyone got along with one another and it was indeed great.

Three years passed by, and life seemed to be running by because we were getting ready to graduate from the eighth grade. Graduation came faster than we expected, and it was all over. Through the summer, we saw each other after which school resumed. At this stage, life was getting ready to change for us as a new chapter was about to be opened, and our alliance was broken into three phases because we all ended up attending different high schools. What is more, we began high school and we couldn't see or speak to one another like before, but we did keep in touch. Since we were not in the same schools, it was a struggle to keep in touch, and the years were moving fast.

One day, years after Mia and I became mutual friends, I received a call from a friend that Mia had just given birth to a baby boy and we should go and see the baby. I was shocked to hear the news. I never believed her and assumed it was a joke, but she assured me that she was telling the truth. We hung up and I ran to inform my mother about the news and she was also surprised. In haste, I ended up catching the nearest bus to Mia's home because I was finding it hard to believe the update about her. Since I and Mia hadn't seen for a long time, I was unaware of her sex life let alone her state of pregnancy. I expected her to have at least called to tell me about her moment of intimacy. I couldn't believe that she had really given birth to a child, but it was true. Mia had a beautiful baby boy when she was two months away from her sixteenth birthday which was in August. Her grandmother and mother talked about their plan to give the baby up for adoption, but Mia refused. Having had this conversation in the presence of the baby's father, made him angry. We decided to leave so as to not be a part of the argument we felt was about to happen.

While visiting her, she shared with us that she lost her virginity right after her fifteenth birthday to a young man named Darryl. He had convinced her to sleep with him while his mother wasn't home. Darryl didn't seem to be someone Mia would like, so this was a surprise to me. She recalled that the experience was not that painful but not enjoyable enough for her to remember details. She believed that she was in love and decided to give in to Darryl's requests without really understanding what sex was all about. Darryl proceeded to tell me how Mia didn't realize that she was pregnant until she was two months away from her delivery and by that time, it was too late to weigh their options. I was astonished as to why she was unable to notice that her waistline was getting bigger. He was kind of upset about their living situation as he wanted far more for Mia and their child. Darryl seemed to have great intentions, as well as, high expectations for him and Mia, and all he spoke of was how to make the future better than their present situation. It was nice to hear a young man at the age of seventeen speak so highly regardless of the backlash of the sex and pregnancy.

Her mother and aunt helped her tremendously with her son and she was truly appreciative. They baby-sat the child for her whenever she went to school or had the need to go out. In contrast, the major issue she had was her finances as it seemed that no one could help her. Her boyfriend assisted her with the baby's needs but he really wasn't prepared to assist her with her personal financial needs. Though she really had great support, she needed much more in every aspect of her life.

By Senior year, her financial issues were made public as she lamented about her mother not having the financial ability to pay for senior activities or fees. This made it hard for her to do a lot of things on which she had her mind. Nevertheless, she continued and ended her last year in high school with dignity despite her home and personal issues.

Graduation had come and gone and Mia was pregnant again. It seemed after all the struggle she had gone through, she had learned nothing. Considering the situation, my thought was that she was just being spiteful toward her mother. The father wasn't excited, but he stuck around. This was a situation she never planned for, but she delivered another baby boy which was just as gorgeous as the first.

At the birth of the second love child, things began to fall apart for Mia and her boyfriend. This was as a result of Mia's suspicion that her boyfriend was cheating on her. She was determined not to have anything to do with him any longer. Like many young men and women in her situation, once separation sets in, they feel they have no responsibility for the children. This was exactly what happened in her situation as he refused to come and see how the kids were doing. On numerous occasions, she would tell him that the children had nothing to do with him being a father and that she would never deprive him of fatherhood. Unfortunately for her, the more she tried, the harder he pulled away and the less he sent money for assistance. Meanwhile, Mia was working, but she wasn't making enough to cater to the needs of the kids. What could be more miserable than being a single mother of two at the age of eighteen? It was really a life altering situation for her. Mia had been helping her mother pay bills, taking care of her two kids and giving a helping hand to her sister and brother. This was too much for her to bear but she was desperate to get back on her feet. She wanted her own place because the house was becoming more crowded with her two kids being added to the existing residents. She returned to school to take general classes while working two jobs. She was concerned about getting a new place so she can perhaps get things moving.

Although she never got the chance to check on her children frequently as a result of her work and school, she still maneuvered her way to spend a little time with them every weekend. She was in pursuit of a better future for her kids and trying all she could to avoid them ending up in an overcrowded environment. Her desperation to make life better prompted her to get up early every morning for work and school and as far as she was concerned, she never complained of tiredness or being upset over school or work. She strongly believed that hard work would pay off sooner or later.

While the relationship with the father of her children became almost non-existent, her personal life became the same. The thought of anyone being with an eighteen-year old with two children seemed uninviting. She went out with a couple of guys but none of them stuck around that long. Whenever she did get a chance to go out, she made sure it was on her terms and that she had to be in control of the relationships. She gave up on finding a special man and decided that casual dating would be best.

Two years passed, and she was still living in the crowded house and her kids were growing bigger. It was becoming more uncomfortable for them to sleep with her. Her life seemed as if it was at a standstill. With the holiday season rolling around the corner, she was clueless of where to get money to get her kids gifts. Even with her two jobs, she couldn't afford a few gifts. I think this was the first time I ever saw her cry as she was extremely broke. She called the kids' father, but the story was just the same. He ultimately managed to get the kids a few things for Christmas. Then five days before Christmas, Mia faced a hard decision which led her experiment with exotic dancing as a stripper. She danced for about four days and made about twelve hundred dollars. She made sure every dime was spent on the kids and vowed never to put herself in such a predicament again. Just when she started saving money in order to move on, something came up at home and she had to empty her savings. She was crushed and felt rejected as the same incident continued to show up that she needed to care for.

Her sour life seemed to be tasting sweet when she ended up being introduced to an Italian man who she wanted to marry for the sake of money. The man liked her, but the marriage could only be possible if he could receive citizenship. This marriage imposed on her beliefs and she was determined to make her first marriage her last but, she needed the money. She began dating but there was a guy who stood out from others that she adored. She was really crazy about him but sadly, the guy ended up moving to Seattle, Washington. During a summer, she spoke with her kids' father about the possibility of the kids staying with him and lo and behold, he agreed. She lied about embarking on a trip to Washington with her friends. While we told her that this was not the best decision at that time, she disregarded our advice and did what she wanted to do. She was really having a great time in Washington, thinking she would send for her kids to permanently reside there. However, Washington was too far from the family that helped her raise the kids despite their issues. All her effort to reside permanently in Washington that summer was futile.

After she returned from Washington, her new boyfriend came back to Chicago with her, where they decided to get a place together. During this time, her grandmother got sick and was admitted to a rehabilitation center. Mia had to stay in her place until she returned home. She made use of her grandmother's apartment with her boyfriend and kids for over a month. While she stayed there, she was searching for a low-income apartment in the surrounding states of Illinois. She was contacted for a place in Iowa, went for an appointment, was approved, and was able to find a place suitable for her and the children. After the return of her grandmother from the hospital, she got on the bus and left Chicago.

This was the beginning of a new dawn for her and she wouldn't trade it for anything else. She moved into her new place, just her and her children. She was happy that she got what she desired most. At her own convenience, she bought the things she needed to furnish her home, one at a time whenever she could afford to get them. Finally, she felt like she made the right decision with her move and she was proud of herself. The kids no longer had to share a space or bed with anyone as each of them had a room to themselves. Her new life in Iowa was great and she started taking classes again at the local college and was working. The kids were in school and they fell so much in love being in their school. She had a boyfriend who was working and helping her out with the children's schedule. Life seemed better off until her boyfriend lost his job and wasn't looking for a new one. After a while, it appeared that he wasn't adjusting very well to the change in their zip codes. Mia was the only one pulling the weight, and she grew tired of his childish antics but never uttered a word of her disappointment to him. She helped him until he found new employment. Mia was very upset because he made a lot of excuses about finding employment because he had more education than others. He was a college graduate, held a bachelor's degree in Engineering but never used it to his advantage. To add insult to injury, he wouldn't stop smoking marijuana. She hoped that he would change or get wiser as he got older.

When Mia's sister decided to move to Iowa to get a fresh start, Mia invited her to come and stay with her. Having her sister living with her made hell break loose in her home as things didn't work well with her sister and her boyfriend. They argued about almost every trivial issue. Mia spoke with her sister to realize that her sister was only trying to protect her from the man who never valued her. Her sister started working where Mia's boyfriend worked and she deliberately befriended a young lady who revealed that she and Mia's boyfriend were seeing one another. Mia's sister became furious that he was dating this girl and at the same time, living with her sister. She confronted him because of his fake and phony nature but he denied the allegation made against him. Mia was informed, and she did nothing about what her sister had told her, instead she acted like nothing happened. Since Mia had no proof of his cheating, she ignored what her sister said in order to allow peace in her home. She continued to go to work and school because she was determined to do what she needed to do.

One day, after work she decided to stay home because there wasn't school that day and to her surprise, she caught her man having a conversation on the phone with another woman. She eavesdropped on their conversation, hearing him tell this woman of his plan to leave Mia and be with her. Mia became upset, confronted him, and this led to a big argument that resulted in him gathering his things and leaving the home. She cried but tried her best not to allow the situation to stop her from what she needed to do for herself and her children. She was greatly hurt by his betrayal, but she moved on as if nothing had happened.

Four weeks after his exit, he returned begging Mia, telling her that he was just misguided and needed someone to spend time with because she was not always at home. Believing him, she agreed to resume the relationship. Having him back home and in her life made her happy and vowed to spend more quality time with him. It was crystal clear from his look that he was a big kid who longed for Mia's attention but no one liked him because of his rude and disrespectful character. Whenever I was on the phone with Mia, he felt as if I called to speak about him and he made comments about our conversations. There were times while we were talking where he would shout so that she would give him her full attention. On several occasions, he would pick up the phone while we were talking and just listen. Their relationship was becoming annoying to people around them and many of her friends stepped away from her as a result of this. He made harsh comments about her new friends tagging them as whores and sluts; Mia was not left out as she was also called a whore whenever she would go out with her co-workers. He never wanted her to go out without his notice and when she did, they would argue for several days. She soon realized how jealous and controlling he was. She couldn't understand why he was acting so jealous. At first, she thought it was insecurity, but realized that he was still with the woman her sister had told her about before. This young lady wanted him all to herself and he couldn't deal with the pressure. The guilt was hitting at his conscience and he could no longer be with Mia without giving up his secret.

After searching through his things, she found out everything. Whenever Mia worked overnight and the kids and her sister were asleep, he would sneak out to this woman's house. This was just the beginning of his deceit, but to make matters worse he was helping his secret girlfriend to pay the bills at her home while Mia struggled to make ends meet thinking that student loans were taking all his money. Finally, Mia went through his phone and found messages from this woman telling him that she was pregnant, and this was the breaking point for Mia. She packed all his things, escorted the items to the woman's home and left everything on the front porch. After he woke up and saw his things missing, he asked her what was going on and Mia let him know what she found.

"Why would you go through my stuff", he asked furiously.

She refused to talk and simply ordered him to leave her home. At first, he refused to leave but when the police arrived, he was forcefully escorted out of her house. His new girlfriend called and told him that his things were at her home. Leaving no stone unturned, Mia took every precaution so as to make sure he no longer had her contact information. She changed her cell and home phone numbers and after a while, he stopped calling and stopped coming by. Mia's heart was torn and her soul was crushed but regardless of this, she continued to go on for the sake of her children.

In addition to the issue she was having at home, her education was becoming a strain on her physically and she felt it was necessary to take a semester off from school which ended up becoming years. Then came an issue with her brother. She learned after calling her brother for his birthday that her mother was unable to provide him with his necessities, such as deodorant and toothpaste. She couldn't understand why her mother couldn't purchase him those things when every month she received a check for his needs, since he was autistic. As a result of this, things got out of hand and she basically went off on her mother. In her fury she let her mother know that if she did not start managing her money correctly, she would come and get her brother and become the overseer of his funds. Her mother's gambling problem was becoming an issue as she wasn't caring for Mia's brother the way she should have done financially. Interestingly, her mother was a skilled carpenter who made huge amounts of money when she worked but she couldn't keep employment. Mia was very close with her siblings and would do anything for their wellbeing no matter who ever got upset with the outcome.

Shortly after Mia's conversation with her mother, she decided to move to Iowa, giving Mia the opportunity to take care of her brother. Mia's sister got her own place. This was a new start for her whole family, and she was excited to have everyone with her. Her mother helped her with the kids, and she was gradually getting over the relationship she ended previously. Once her mother moved, so did her grandfather. Although she didn't know he was a part of the move, it was too late to tell him no. Mia's problem with her grandfather being there was that he had a drinking problem and was a deadbeat to her mother and his other kids. Nevertheless, they were now all living together. She couldn't understand why her mother would want him there even if he didn't have anywhere else to go. She just sucked up her pride and handled the situation.

Soon after her mother packed into her home, things started to spiral downward financially because the gambling was consistent and becoming a real reality in Mia's life. The bills were coming up and some bills weren't getting paid and she felt her life was tumbling fast. She tried her best to speak with her mother about her gambling problem, but she did not change. It got even worse when Mia's mother took her bank card and withdrew money about six times at an ATM in the casino. This upset Mia because she was trying to pay a bill but her card had been denied due to her what her mother did. Mia had worked so hard to get the things she wanted and in just a couple of months, her mother threw everything she worked for in the garbage. She sold her television in order to get money for her mother to pay for rent and phone bill. Later, she learned from the landlord that her mother had not paid the rent. Mia couldn't bear her mother's antics and decided that moving out to get another place would be the best option for her. Mia left her mother's place and decided to share a place with her sister. The arrangement with her sister was great although there were a few arguments every once in a while. The kids needed a stable environment and her sister had just had her baby and she needed Mia's help and advice. More and more, her comfortable living situation allowed her more free time which led her to jump back into the dating scene.

Dating was very hard for her because she was a single parent. She decided not to take anyone seriously and chose to date casually and have a good time. This approach of dating didn't last long because everyone she met always seemed to want more than she was willing to offer. She ended up making several bad choices and sex became the next level in the casual dating scene. She tried to refrain but she was having sex just for the sake of enjoyment. She never wanted her body to be for fun alone, but this experience of casual dating led to causal sex for her.

While out at night, she met a man named Bryan. He was a dark-skinned man with small eyes and dark lips. He was a little shorter than Mia due to his average height. They were out at a party and he came and asked Mia for a dance and she agreed. After the dance, they chatted for hours and by the end of the night, they knew so much about one another. Bryan was a successful engineer who had no children, but he had his own home and a car. They exchanged numbers and went their separate ways for the night. This was a dream come true for Mia as she never thought of meeting a man like Bryan again in her life. Mia decided to call him before she went to sleep, and they had a long phone conversation talking until the sun came up. They liked each other and decided to meet one another for lunch that same day. As the time for them to meet drew near, she was overanxious. She had never been like this over a man. They met at a small restaurant, had a great lunch and their conversation went from her goals to her children. She was amazed that someone could be so interested in her and the kids. Although she thought the man was God sent, she decided to take things slowly.

Naturally, she couldn't stick to the slow process of getting to know him mentally and spiritually without indulging in physical activities. Since she felt like it was the right man for her, she gave herself to him. They decided that they were going to be in a monogamous relationship together. Bryan lived a few blocks away from her and she spent every weekend at his home, and on some occasions, she took the kids with her. The way he interacted with the children made her happy; he treated them as if they were his own children. The children were excited to have a man around with consistency and she felt like she had met the man of her dream. Six months into their relationship, the discussion of marriage had come up so fast and her thought was that maybe he will be asking her for her hand in marriage very soon. As she pondered on what could be best for their relationship, Bryan received a job offer in St. Louis, Missouri. He spoke with her regarding the new promotion and relocation and they decided that the promotion would be the best decision for him. She was so consumed with her feelings regarding this promotion that he felt like she wasn't happy for him. Despite her reaction, he asked about the possibility of her and the kids moving out of the state with him. She declined his offer after deep thought and conversations with her family members. Bryan was crushed and couldn't grasp why she wouldn't go with him but he never argued or fought her on her decision.

Two months after he accepted the promotion, he allowed his sister to stay in his home because he didn't want to sell the house. Mia went over and helped him pack everything he needed to take along. This took a couple of days and as a result of this, they had a great time enjoying each other's company before he finally moved. The weekend was over and Mia tried her best to hide her feelings because it was time for Bryan to leave. The movers had finished loading the truck and Bryan was driven to the airport. The ride to the airport was silent as neither of them dared to break the silence in the car. They reached the airport, stepped out of the car and kissed, holding each other as if for the last time. While they both cried, Bryan made it known that Mia could come to be with him anytime she wanted.

Bryan came home after a month and she was so excited to see him. She missed him dearly and they spent the weekend together. But something was different about the way he looked at her and he couldn't think that she had changed so much in a month. He didn't hold her or even speak to her like he used to. She never bothered to ask him why things seemed so different between them, instead, she decided to let the weekend play itself out. They spent every single day of his stay together despite what she was feeling. As soon as the weekend ended, they parted with a kiss and went their ways. It was during his visit that they made plans about Valentine's Day.

They talked through text and emails on a regular basis but as time went on, the phone calls seemed to disappear slowly. Mia couldn't put her hands on what was going on and she decided to wait until she went to visit him on Valentine's Day. The weekend came sooner than she expected and the day before she left, she decided to check his 'My Space' page. While observing his page, she found a comment from a young lady from St. Louis stating that, "You may have had him once but he's mine." Mia didn't know what the young lady meant by the comment but she was very upset about it. She called Bryan to ask if he was dating this young lady or sleeping with her. He tried to lie but when she pressured him, he told the truth about having sex with her. He begged Mia not to be upset and told her that loneliness was the reason why he had slept with her. He stressed the fact that he really needed someone, and this young lady was always sticking around. Mia refused to accept this as an excuse for him to cheat on her and at that moment in time, she made it known that she would no longer want to be a part of his life. That was the end of the promising relationship between Mia and Bryan.

Back to square one, Mia's love life wasn't going as planned. The kids were getting older and she had to be careful about the men she brought around. She knew she was getting older and she wanted to lead by example as she didn't want her boys to see their mother with different men. She simply wanted their respect. The years after her relationship with Bryan ended, were not very good for Mia. She reached a dead end when she found out that the apartment she shared with her sister was getting ready to be sold. Mia took it upon herself to look for an apartment but after searching for several weeks, she was unsuccessful in securing one and the moving date drew close. Unfortunately for Mia, she had to call her mother to ask if they could move in with her so they could save money to get a place. Despite the fact that the home was extremely cramped, they decided to go ahead with the move. Mia knew this wasn't a living style she wanted especially for the kids even though she lived like that before.

Mia ended up living with her mom for about a year and she continuously stumbled into issues that halted her growth. Moreover, her mom was back to her old antics of 'wanting and needing' money. She was starting to feel the heartache that she once felt when she was a child. One day, as she was exiting the home, her mother's landlord stopped and asked about the rent. Mia had given her mother the money for the rent at the beginning of the month. Mia knew her mom had spent the money and after confronting her she learned that the money was gone. Her mother had gambled the money away and Mia was tired and very disappointed yet again. Her mother was getting worse and she wasn't going to stop as long as she had the help of her children.

Mia knew it was time to leave and she had a plan to leave Iowa once and for all by saving every dollar she could to better her living situation. After six months, she had saved ten thousand dollars. She rented a car and moved to California where she found two jobs and returned to school. Ultimately, she graduated from hair school and planned to open her own salon. Her children embraced their new environment and she finally found the man she had been waiting for.

At long last, through the thick and thin, Mia is now back to school and currently working on helping and rebuilding her community.

Same Shoes Different Paths

Volume 2

Marquita D. Dorsey

WEAPONS
OF
MASS
SYDNEY

Sydney and I met during my freshman year in high school. She had big brown beautiful eyes and a round face fancied by the prettiest dimples. She was kind of thick, not skinny, and always had the newest shoes and a designer purse to match. Although there were four of us who hung out together, Sydney and I were closer than the other girls. We became friends almost instantly and had all our classes together.

By sophomore year, we were close enough for a sleepover. However, my father did not permit me to stay at Sydney's house until he spoke with her parent. It was after my arrival that I realized she lived with her aunt. Sydney was the middle child on her mother's side, having an older brother and a younger sister. Secretly, I wondered why she didn't live with her mother, but I never asked, believing I would know the reason in due time.

After spending several nights with Sydney, I learned that her brother and sister lived with their grandmother on the next block. Their grandma had a beautiful home with six bedrooms, and while visiting her one day, the mystery of Sydney not living with her mom was solved. It all unraveled when their mother stopped by the grandma's house, and through a series of events, I learned she was addicted to crack cocaine.

Besides her mom's personal issues, she seemed great to me, displaying an up-front attitude and a bubbling personality. Though Sydney and her mother didn't look alike, they had the same bright smile and beautiful dimples. She had a functioning relationship with both her parents, but these relationships weren't everything she wanted them to be. Nevertheless, they were still better than what others expected under the circumstances.

As time progressed, Sydney would lose her virginity a month before she told anyone. The young man responsible was the same age as her and bore the name Joseph. Joseph was a boy she had known all her life, and it appeared they had been in a relationship since the beginning of freshman year. By the time the second semester of our sophomore year rolled around, Sydney was pregnant. She was about two months along when she shared the news with me. I was shocked at first and couldn't believe it. What a reality check!

Apparently, the child's father was not Joseph, but instead, another man she had been dating for a while. This young man attended high school with us but was a year older. His name was Terry, and he was a light-skinned, big head guy with Chinese-like eyes and a huge smile. Though deemed a class clown, he always stayed fresh when it came to the latest fashions. Outside of school, he was an average young man who stood by the corner.

For a while, things weren't perfect, but they weren't complicated either. That is until Sydney found out that Terry wasn't pleased with her pregnancy. The reason why was because he was dating someone else. Furthermore, he had impregnated another girl, and

Same shoes different paths

due to his predicament, he didn't want Sydney to bear his child. Therefore, she became quite impatient with him and decided to move on with her life. But "moving on" included telling her aunt about the pregnancy and the horrible circumstances surrounding this situation.

Now that I look back, I damn well believe her confession was the breaking point of her living with her aunt because soon after, she moved back to her grandmother's house. There, she struggled daily with what she would do regarding the child she was carrying. It wasn't until her second trimester that she finally decided not to have the baby. However, she couldn't find any place in the city willing to terminate the pregnancy because, at this stage, an abortion would jeopardize her health. Sydney ended up driving about an hour away from home to receive a two-day procedure and spent about a thousand dollars to achieve her goal. She was scorned for the decision she made but knew it was the best decision for her future.

After returning to school, it seemed like my friend was never really the same girl. Most days, she was late getting to class, and sometimes, she made matters worse by not showing up at all. I saw her less and less throughout our sophomore year because she found pleasure in staying away from school. Sydney's academic decline became evident in the downward spiral of her grades. In short, she had changed, and it wasn't for the better.

Outside of Sydney's circumstances, the rest of us excitedly awaited our summer break. What none of us looked forward to was being away from one another for so long.

Time seemed to fly by, and before we knew it, summer was over. We were now juniors and very excited to see one another again. Unfortunately, soon after the first semester, Sydney was back to her old habit of missing school. By February, she wasn't showing up at all, and because of this pitiful pattern, she ultimately dropped out. Surprisingly, Sydney called me one day to tell me that she was pregnant again, and this time, she decided to keep the child. The ill-effects of the last abortion had scared her away from repeating the process. Plus, she suffered from terrifying nightmares that made her stand by her decision.

Despite peoples' concerns about her becoming a sixteen-year-old mother, she found herself a job working at a daycare center as a teacher's aide. She worked up until the day she went into labor, and that October, she had a baby boy who was cute with big dimples. Though the father wasn't there when she had her son, they continued to date one another. Then, just four months later, Sydney found out she was pregnant again.

Sincerely shocked, she really couldn't believe that she had gotten herself into this situation all over again. Nine months later, precisely in the month of October, she had a baby girl. Her son and daughter were just a couple of days apart. Her little girl was just as cute as her son. Sadly, the father of her children didn't accept the little girl as being his. Sydney was crushed because she knew that her children had the same father. Unfortunately, his error marked the beginning of the end of their relationship.

When she decided to move on, the father started making a difference in how he treated the children. For instance, he would come and pick up his son, leaving his daughter behind. Sydney continued to allow him to spend time with their son so the two of them could build a relationship.

Being eighteen with two kids, she thought she would never find a new man. Fortunately for her, she reunited with someone she grew up with. His name was Twon, and he was short, dark-skinned, round-faced with slanted eyes. When she fell for this man, she fell hard. He was a little younger than she was, but his age didn't matter to her. Sydney loved this guy because he treated her well and even paid her kids a lot of attention. She felt that this attention and having a man around was something her children needed.

This guy was getting money legally and illegally and had two children of his own, with two different girls. Nevertheless, she didn't let the fact that he had children interfere with their relationship. It wasn't long before Sydney became pregnant, but this time she decided against having another baby. She reasoned with herself, asking what she would do with another child. Therefore, she told no one of this pregnancy and hid it to the best of her ability.

After raising the abortion money, she went and terminated the pregnancy. She felt drained after this abortion but didn't allow it to keep her down and continued with her life. In time Sydney knew she had made the right decision because she got a phone call from one of his son's mother, telling her that they were still together. Afterward, Sydney was hurt and couldn't believe that she was back in the same boat once again. Twon was a cheater, and his cheating had become a part of their relationship. Though she confronted him, he really didn't have much to say; as a matter of fact, he didn't deny the accusations.

Sydney loved this guy, and she utilized the time she could spare to spend time with him either by going to the movies or just being together at her home. They laughed, got drunk, and made love every possible chance they had.

However, it wasn't long before his baby mama became overbearing with phone calls to Sydney, telling her everything she did with Twon. Luckily, Sydney was a doctor junkie and kept regular appointments. During a checkup, she found out that she had an STD and was furious that the doctor had to prescribe medication to cure her. She then called Twon and asked what was going on, but he had nothing to say other than apologizing.

It wasn't long after her phone conversation with Twon that she received a call from his baby mama. Sydney was growing tired of this whole threesome situation, but Twon made it clear with his actions that his baby mama would be a part of his life regardless of what anyone said!

Sydney was upset but resigned to play along, so she did not lose him. With all her heartache and pain, she continued to work while supporting her kids. The children's father wasn't doing much of anything for them, not even calling or coming by to see them.

It would be safe to say he forgot that they existed.

Despite Sydney's efforts to make him a better father, he declined and didn't want to be involved with her or the kids. Sadly, this situation never improved. However, Sydney tried her best to make life more meaningful by planning enjoyable activities for the children.

While Sydney was at work, her mother and Grandmother watched over her children. Her grandmother was always loving and supportive of any move she wanted to make; regardless of her bad decisions, she would never judge her. Sydney loved and appreciated her grandmother for all she did, and they had a great relationship. Unfortunately, Sydney never returned for the remainder of high school. She just worked and tried to make things easier for herself.

Following my graduation, we ended up hanging out with each other daily. Then, one day, out of the blue, Sydney decided to get her GED. She was very excited when she received her diploma and felt nothing could slow her down. They continued to live with her grandmother, occupying one side of the basement while her mother occupied the other. By the time she was twenty, her life had started gathering momentum and heading in a positive direction. Things even started getting a little better for her financially, and personally then, tragedy hit her hard. In November, Sydney's Grandmother passed away, which caused her to fall into a deep depression. Sadly, like almost everyone else in her family, she didn't know how to function without the love and support of her grandmother.

Like in many other families, her grandma was a black, strong, and great woman, otherwise known as "the rock," of the family. I accompanied her to the funeral for support, and I don't regret it at all. I loved her grandmother, and I always will. Right after her grandmother's death (not even a month or two later), she was forced out of her home.

Her aunt, who was head of the estate, decided that everyone needed to leave, what she referred to as the "comfort zone of her mother's home."

This directive was something I don't think Sydney was ready for, but the reality was she had to live by it. As fate would have it, she was not the only one forced out; her cousin shared in the exit saga as well. Due to their finances, Sydney and her cousin decided to combine their resources and get an apartment together. They ended up renting a two-bedroom apartment with a dining room and living room. Everything about this new apartment was really nice, including the hardwood floors. She converted the dining room into a bedroom for the kids, and her mother did sleep in the living room whenever she came over.

Being that Sydney was still in mourning, the added stress pushed her into a state of needing someone who would never judge her but opened their arms to love her. The lack thereof, coupled with all the forced changes, sparked a new flame in her, and it wasn't for the best. She now devoted her nights to drinking Hennessey, vodka, and Remy to whatever she could get her hands on. At this point in her life, she drank so much because she couldn't deal with reality. Her boyfriend wasn't much help; he didn't even show up for the funeral and began to see her less and less. One of his baby's mothers started calling her phone, questioning her about her relationship with her baby's father.

Alas, she'd had enough and wasn't going to accept this headache any longer! As long as she was insecure about his fidelity in their relationship, she had no problem moving on, and that's what she did.

Unfortunately, the failed relationship deepened her weakness for alcohol. Drinking boosted her confidence, making her feel a little worthy, but I could tell she was no longer happy with herself. She often questioned her grandmother's death, and although she was still seeing Twon, they were no longer in a relationship. It seemed everyone she loved was leaving her, and Sydney could no longer handle the pressure of being alone. Alcohol helped her avoid these issues, so she began to drink even more.

Her home had become the hang-out for drinking, smoking, and partying. It took her about two months to find a new man, but this new man couldn't stop her from holding on to the old one. He was a little younger than the old one, but like his predecessor he was a hustler, but this didn't stop her from being with him. He bought her a ring, and she opened her home to his mother and sister, treating them like family.

After a while, and like the other men she dated, he decided he wanted to be with someone else. Sydney couldn't stop herself from drinking to alleviate the pain. After the breakup, she felt compelled to return to her previous boyfriend, who manipulated her into a late-night romance. At home, the year-long living arrangement between Sydney and her cousin came to an end when the cousin decided to move out. The transition left her and the kids in a horrible situation. She knew she couldn't afford the apartment, lights, and gas without the financial help of someone else. How many times would she be forced out of her home due to someone else's decision, she thought.

After trying to survive on her own, she ended up moving in with one of her cousins and his girlfriend. She put her bed in their living room for her and the kids to sleep and lived out of plastic bags for two months before finding a new place to live.

I went to visit her one day, and we went outside while the kids were asleep. During this time, she began to drink, and as we reminisced, tears rolled down her round face because she could no longer hold her pain inside. I told her to let it out, and she said that she wanted her grandmother. She talked about the aftermath of her grandmother's passing and how it made her feel like the walls were closing in on her. She shared that life had never been this hard before, even though she struggled since she was much younger.

Sydney's grandmother showed her that family was the best support she could ever have, but after she died, it seemed that her family had become distant from one another. Now, Sydney couldn't handle the dysfunction because she was used to everyone being together.

I assured her that life would be whatever she wanted it to be regardless of the past and that she could be the force that everyone needed to be whole once again. With that motivation, she dried her tears, and we embraced one another. I reassured her that I would be there no matter what and asked her to call me if she needed anything. I believe our talk helped her gather her thoughts and gave her a positive outlook.

Soon after her 22nd birthday, she acquired a new apartment that everyone adored. The kids had their own room, and her mother alternated living with her and her brother, but she stayed with her most of the time. With her mother being there, Sydney knew it was the perfect opportunity to attend school. Therefore, she signed up for a medical assistance course which would take a few months to complete. This new path was all Sydney needed to take her mind off her relationship problems. Plus, she had a new job that was kind enough to schedule her work hours after class.

I don't know if, along the way, she started to feel down again, but some days, she just didn't feel like going to class. She never flunked out, and when she studied, she did well, but only when she applied herself.

At last, she graduated and was very excited to have accomplished this important goal. Unfortunately, after graduation, she was unable to secure a job in the field. Even worse, to attend this class, Sydney had to take out a ten-thousand-dollar loan because she didn't qualify for financial aid. The rules stated that if Sydney didn't qualify after six months of receiving her certification, she had to start paying off her loan immediately regardless of her income. This loan made her suffer more financial setbacks, and more than ever, the kid's father needed to step up and be a part of their lives. Although he had been inactive in their lives for a while now, the thought of him doing so perished when she found out he was incarcerated. His family would call every now and then, but only to see about her son. Being fed up with them and their antics, she decided not to accept this treatment from their father or his family any longer. She advised him that if he felt like he couldn't be a father to both their kids, he needed to get a blood test.

No longer would she allow him or his family to divvy love and affection to one child and not the other. He apologized for the division and said that he would try harder to be a great parent to both kids. She thanked him and reassured him that she would bring the kids to spend time with him once he returned home.

After completing his sentence, he had the kids at his house only a couple of times before bailing again. Sydney had to admit it was more than he had been doing, but it still she wasn't enough- she was done making excuses for his shortcomings. With everything that happened in her life the last couple of years, she began to resent everything and everyone around her.

Right after her birthday, one of the worst storms Chicago had seen in years hit the area in full force. During this time, Sydney's mother called, frantically informing her daughter that she was being evicted. Even as they spoke, workers from the sheriff's department put her belongings out on the curb. She then called me to share her plight and how she had been desperately struggling, even to the point of applying for rental assistance. Unfortunately, the landlord didn't want to wait for the payment and proceeded with the eviction. Seeing all the beautiful things her grandmother had given her, the kid's beds, and all she'd worked so hard to get out on the street in the rain was devastating.

At that moment in her life, she gave up and had no fight left in her. She just bowed and asked GOD what she had done for her and the children to continue struggling. Sydney wanted her kids to have a better life than she did, but no matter how hard she tried, she couldn't get out of this hole. After speaking with GOD, she returned home and made a phone call to an old coworker who agreed to help her. His kindness gave her assurance that there was light even in the darkness. He assisted by putting the majority of her things in a storage facility.

Now, the only thing she contemplated was where she and the kids would stay. Her friend let her know that there was an available room for rent in one of the buildings he owned. Sydney was upset and embarrassed but in no condition to let this offer pass her by. She and the children moved into this room immediately after learning of its availability. When they had to share a kitchen and bathroom with someone else, she quickly realized this environment was not what she wanted for her children.

Sydney started to relate angrily to the people around her because she was forced into a world she wasn't ready for. She knew if her grandmother were still alive, she wouldn't be in this predicament. Although she was stressed and disappointed, she went on living and continued to work to make ends meet.

I knew Sydney was a good person and that God was preparing her for something great. It wasn't long after living in this room that she decided to move into another aunt's house. This aunt had a son who lived with her as well. Shortly after Sydney and the kids moved in, her aunt decided to move out, leaving the apartment to Sydney and her son. These arrangements seemed to be a great idea! Sydney and the kids liked the apartment, and she got along well with her cousin. They were happy campers for a couple of months, and she even gave her kids a birthday party at their new humble abode.

The day eventually came when their happiness hit a brick wall. It happened when she used her cousin's car, and he felt she was gone too long with his vehicle. After they argued about it, he hit her in the eye like she was a grown man. As a result, her eye was swollen shut and turned black. More importantly, he had knocked down her pride in the process- She was now wearing the pain she felt so deep inside for the whole world to see.

She knew that it was the pain and alcohol her cousin was feeling ever since the death of their grandmother that had him on edge. However, she couldn't believe that he had gotten that upset over a vehicle that he knew she would return. His abuse was a wake-up call that caused her to save her money and move into a new apartment.

Before she moved, her mother decided to enter rehab. It would seem that Sydney's path made her mother see her own life a little differently. The rehab facility was purposely a thousand miles away from her family and friends to ensure a fresh new start. Sydney talked to her mother regularly, which inspired her to overcome or at least change the way she saw the world and herself.

After about four months, her mother returned home looking refreshed and energetic-She had undoubtedly changed for the better. She got a job and lived in her own apartment with a male friend of hers. She tried her best not to hang around the people with whom she did drugs in the past. I don't know how long it took before she relapsed into her addiction to crack cocaine- but she did. Yet, through it all, she continued to be employed while she took drugs.

Same shoes different paths

The relapse hurt Sydney, but she felt like she could no longer carry everyone else's issues on her shoulders. She had to focus on herself and the children. So, from that moment onward, she continued caring about and loving everyone, but she didn't put their needs in front of her children. Only God would come first because He was her personal Lord and Savior. Sydney moved into the new apartment and thought it was just enough for her and the kids. God had finally answered her prayers by providing for her needs and giving her a place to call her own.

Having a roof, heat, food, and lights in a house they could call their own made her cry the first night she was there due to the joy she felt. Though it wasn't much to those outside looking in, it meant the world to her and the children. She knew the kid's happiness was all she needed to make it through another day. For many years to come, the two-bedroom, one-bath apartment provided the peace of mind for which Sydney had been searching.

Although she was having a great experience with her children physically and emotionally, she was falling apart spiritually. Her job brought her little to no fulfillment because she longed to do something else with her life. Sometimes, she looked in the mirror and didn't recognize who was looking back. Casual dating was no longer satisfying and made her rethink her non-commitment clause. She was longing for something that wasn't there (a real relationship and fulfillment). But instead of seeking someone or something new, she was drinking and continuing to make bad choices.

Her self-respect had diminished, and she no longer considered her life a priority. All these things were evident as she partied all the time and, like her mother, remained involved with the wrong crowd. Even more disturbing was that she repeatedly argued with other females over men. I told her she was worth much more than the company she was keeping and the actions she was taking. Nevertheless, she continued to hang with these girls and be involved in things she never did before. I let her know that this wasn't the crowd she needed to be around if she wanted a change in her life.

Finally, Sydney got the picture and began to pull away from the foolishness. As usual, she was working but this time two hours away from home via public transportation. With her mother not being 100% reliable, she left the kids down the street at their cousin's house. After a year, she was fired and once again placed in an unwanted predicament. At least this time, she would receive unemployment benefits- It wouldn't pay everything; therefore, she subsidized her compensation with government assistance. This way, she and her children would have plenty of food to eat. Something was better than nothing, and she knew her situation could be worse, so she did not complain about the loss of her job.

Being at home allowed her to address personal issues like feeling inadequate and abandoned. After a while, she began to uncover her self-worth and blossom spiritually, making her a better parent. She learned to set boundaries and became more selective about who she dated. The latter earned her more respect from men who had not treated her well in the past.

Same shoes different paths

My childhood friend began to glow, simply by finding herself instead of looking for a man to define her. That's right-Once she stopped looking for love, she found it. The love she wanted wasn't with the man she thought it would be nor the kid's father or even Twon, who she still saw from time to time. Love and beauty had finally sprouted in the eyes of the person who was staring back at her in the mirror.

I remember telling her that she just had to work on herself before she tried to work on a relationship with a man, and I was ecstatic that she took my advice!

When he entered her life, she was working on rebuilding herself, and he didn't impose. He allowed her to be who she was and appreciated who she was becoming. He came around just to build a relationship with her kids. This man was different, he knew about her past and what she wanted in the future, and his actions persuaded her to date and eventually love him. He did not want to just be with her; he wanted to enjoy her kids as well. His love for them grew stronger and stronger every day. Soon he proposed, and she accepted immediately. Not once did he judge her, which made her feel more like the woman she was destined to be.

A few months after their engagement, her fiancé became her husband. Sydney was ecstatic and finally felt the stability she'd longed for since her grandmother passed away. The wedding ceremony was at the city hall, and she invited as many people as possible. Sydney's life fittingly fulfills the proverb; "At the end of a tunnel, there is always a light."

Sydney is now working and continuing her education. The kids are in school and getting excellent grades. Their father is still coming around periodically when he feels the need, and the number of friends who have access to her life is limited. Instead, she chooses to focus on her home rather than what's going on outside. Lastly, Sydney continues to give her mother and relatives love and support and advises all young women that the road will surely get rough, but they should never lose their focus.

**WORLD
WAR 2
BRITTANY**

Brittany is a young lady who I grew up with in my neighborhood. She is light-skinned, or as we say, "high yellow," like the color of the sun. Her large lips sit prominently beneath almond-shaped eyes and a crown of dark shoulder-length hair. Down below, she was thick and curvaceous with a big behind and a healthy set of hips. Brittany loved wearing long, neon-colored nails with rhinestones and huge earrings, but when she tried to move around with the freshest brand-name gear, she fell painfully short. The truth was, Brittany, didn't come from the hood but wanted desperately to belong.

As a matter of fact, Brittany was raised in a two-parent home, being the middle child of five siblings. The family resided in a three-bedroom apartment on the first floor of a two-flat building. From a distance all appeared to be well, but up close the truth was painful. Their home was an overcrowded wreck, the kitchen floor was caved in, and the house had pests. This low standard of living would make any child disturbed and dysfunctional.

When Brittany was twelve years old, she started noticing the mental and verbal abuse her father inflicted upon her mother. He hadn't worked for many years and was supposedly waiting on a settlement check that never arrived. The settlement involved a claim he made against his former employer several years prior. But in reality, Brittany's father was a con artist whose schemes were apparent to everyone who knew him. He often took Brittany's mother's food stamp card to buy other women food. In addition to his heinous negligence, he would force her mother to go grocery shopping on the bus, saying his car couldn't hold fat people!

Nevertheless, her mother stayed, trying to make the best out of what they had. But his behavior only got worse; he started locking the refrigerator with a chain and a padlock. Sometimes, he would buy takeout food and eat in front of the kids while they salivated. At one point, the older children got summer jobs, and he took their meager savings and spent them frivolously. Their mother appeared powerless beneath their father's unyielding abuse; he often called her a slut and a whore in front of the children.

Eventually, Brittany started disrespecting her mother as well because she knew there would be no consequences. Her theory was put to the test when her mother told her she was eating too much junk food. Brittany retorted that she was just jealous because she didn't have her girlish figure. The lack of respect spilled over onto her siblings as Brittany was permitted to cuss and fight with them whenever she saw fit.

Her mother was noticeably overwhelmed and finding it hard to cope. Furthermore, her weak intervention tactics were wasted on her troubled daughter's behavior- things were just too much for her to bear. Then one fateful day when Brittany's mother wasn't home, she and her father got into a verbal altercation resulting in her being admitted into a psychiatric facility. As soon as her mother caught wind of the news, she went to the facility to see how she was faring and if she could take her home. Unfortunately, the situation required Brittany to undergo a two-week evaluation.

Same shoes different paths

Now, we all knew that she wasn't crazy, just a little fast, but crazy – no, not at all.

Doctors questioned and drugged Brittany while she was facilitated, and after two weeks of intense therapy, she was still unable to come home. The Prozac she was given rendered her incompetent and unable to complete her daily tasks.

This incident proved to be the breaking point of an already flimsy relationship between her and her mother. The reason being her mom ended up back at home with a man who had her sent to a mental institution and who continued to disrespect them both!

Besides, her father was plotting to drug them both up with Prozac, but he felt like it would hurt her mother more than helped her.

This insane household dynamic caused Brittany to weigh her options, which were few. Luckily, a great aunt learned of the shenanigans Brittany's mother allowed in their home and decided to take Brittany in.

However, things were different there. Back at home with her parents, she could almost get away with murder, but in her aunt's house, there were rules she had to abide by. And although she was content, the rules were stifling, making her feel like she didn't have the necessary room to grow. So, she contacted the social worker and asked if she could leave because she no longer liked the home where she was staying. Once she was given the green light by the social worker, she moved into another aunt's house on the Westside of Chicago.

Her new aunt and two cousins, Meesha and Treesha, welcomed her with open arms. They knew ahead of time that Brittany was a drama queen, so they let her know upon arriving that they weren't going to disrespect her. This made Brittany feel secure enough to let her guard down and trust that she would love her aunt's place and the new school she would attend.

Unfortunately, it wasn't long before this arrangement fell apart. School began only a week after she arrived, and the teachers were calling already. It seemed Brittany had no problem telling her teachers what she wasn't going to do. This caused them not to be very fond of her. Likewise, the students weren't accepting her bad behavior either- she was always getting into fights with boys and girls. Soon after, her aunt called to inform Brittany's mother about her terrible conduct in school. It really didn't matter, the more her mother chastised her, the more troublesome she became. An important point to remember is that her mother was still going through issues with her father. She couldn't take care of everyone, so she forgot about herself.

In the mean-time, the aunt had reached her breaking point over one incident in particular. It was when a man told Meesha that he was going to buy shorty a pair of shoes and she would give him her body in return. Since Meesha didn't know who he was talking about, she asked, and he described her and gave her Brittany's number. Meesha couldn't believe her cousin was asking people for shoes and compensating them with sex!

Soon after confirming this information, Meesha confronted Brittany, who flat-out denied the accusation. She ranted about how she wasn't going to be accused of something she didn't do. Then, she immediately called her mother and told her she was ready to come home because everyone was being mean and calling her a whore! Her mother came over, gathered Brittany's things, and took her home against the social worker's judgment.

Soon after returning to her parent's home, Brittany turned fourteen. Her home life wasn't getting any better, especially her relationship with her father. A month passed, and out of the blue several young ladies busted out her mother's front window.

"They were jealous of me," Brittany insisted!

All the same, her mother heard both sides of the story and knew her daughter was lying. One of the ladies said that Brittany had slept with her boyfriend and gave him oral sex. Her mother was upset because she thought that Brittany and the young lady were friends. These young ladies continued to accuse and bully Brittany, and her reputation grew worse. Not to mention, her father found some letters that Brittany wrote to a young man stating how much she loved him and that she only cheated one time. She said she didn't mean to cheat on him and that it just happened and that if he loved her, he would forgive her.

During this period, Brittany started staying out all night and coming home at 2 am in the morning. This caused her parents much heartache. This behavior, however, was parallel to her father having everyone in family therapy. His goal was to get everyone on drugs so he could be the overseer of the government checks. This was his clever idea, so he would never have to work again.

Heart-wrenching, as well, was the time before Christmas when everyone was away from home except the mother and her youngest child.

After waiting a while for his mom to prepare his food, he entered the kitchen. To his shocking surprise, he found her lying on the floor – it was a coma situation. He called 911, and an ambulance rushed her to the hospital. A few days after her admission and running several tests, the doctors couldn't find out what was wrong with her. A trach tube was then inserted into her neck, rendering her unable to speak. Nine days later, the doctors diagnosed her with Lupus. She remained in the ICU for a month.

Afterward, she was transferred to a rehabilitation center to learn how to walk and talk again.

It hurt Brittany to see her mother unable to do the things she used to do so easily. Unfortunately, within a month of her mother's return home, it was still the same story of fighting, arguing, and disrespecting all over again! Their home tumbled more and more out of control as Brittany's older brother moved out because of the unceasing uproar. Then the final straw that broke the family's back was a dispute between Brittany and her father over her coming in late. This resulted in a hollering match that was loud enough to wake the neighbors. In his rage, Brittany's father called her a slut and a whore, crushing her mentally and emotionally! Regardless of her pain, she continued to argue, hoping to get him to like or even acknowledge her, but he never did.

Before she knew it, the fight escalated from verbal confrontation to physical combat. Brittany was terrified because her father began choking her and telling her that he deserved her respect. She began to gasp for air while trying to break his grasp from her neck, and in the process, he scratched her. After rolling around and tussling for a while, he finally let her go, and she jumped out the window and went to her cousin's house.

Once Brittany explained what happened and the cousin confirmed the story by the bruises she sustained, she contacted the police, and this led to the arrest of her father. Sadly, when the police questioned the mother (who was in the home), she said she didn't witness anything, and the charges were dropped.

Brittany felt like she couldn't go back home because her father didn't like her, and her mother was delusional. So, at sixteen, she moved in with her cousin, who had a daughter a year older than her. The seventeen-year-old was allowed to have her boyfriend spend the night. This was a foreign concept for Brittany, but she couldn't run someone else's household, so she decided to say nothing. It wasn't long after that her older cousin became pregnant.

Two months later, her mother decided to separate from her husand and take her two youngest children. She told Brittany where to meet her, and they were off. Her mother really didn't have a plan, so they ended up at her grandmother's home. Now the grandmother had a three-bedroom apartment with five people occupying it. However, Brittany's grandma welcomed them with open arms. Soon the apartment was so overcrowded that difficulties started to arise.

When Brittany's mother and father separated, it was May, and school was almost over. By then, Brittany had found herself a new boyfriend whose name was Horace. She was bringing him around regularly, and no one seemed to notice that this young man never talked about attending school. He was a tall, light-skinned, young, goofy, and childish man who wore the latest fashions with a peanut head and a dimple in his chin. After I met him, I thought they were perfect for one another-yet; I was concerned that they were young and naive about life and its consequences.

After Horace became more familiar with our family, he told Brittany's aunt that he was twenty-one years old. Meaning there was a six-year age gap between them. She kept his actual age a secret because she knew that there would be some resistance from her family. Brittany's mother, however, understood Horace was older than her daughter and that he could be jailed for statutory rape. But because of her personal issues, the mother decided to let her daughter enjoy the illegal companionship. Now Brittany always had decent grades in school and never let her actions stop her from progressing, but maintaining mediocre grades wasn't the issue. There were constant calls from her teachers about her unruly and disrespectful attitude. She seemed to wither away from rules no matter what environment she was in.

After a while, she started spending nights out like she was a grown woman and coming home from school at two or three in the morning. As soon as her mother began to tell her that her behavior was unacceptable, she devised a way to sneak Horace into the house. They could be found sleeping anywhere, be it on the living room or kitchen floor, just as long as they were together.

The two showed blatant disregarded for their actions and all who witnessed them, including the children. However, after several sexual encounters, Horace no longer wanted to be committed to her, which broke Brittany's heart. Unfortunately, Brittany was one of those young ladies who always had to get burned to learn, and she got burned quite often- listening was not her strong suit.

Horace began coming by when he wanted and answered her calls when he felt the need. He was literally giving her the runaround. Even worse, she knew he was cheating on her, and he no longer lied about his activities. Brittany's heart was crushed, and they argued back and forth. She called him a whore, and his only response was that he didn't mean to put her life at risk, and he was sorry.

After a week of heated phone calls, she refused to answer, let alone speak to him. She believed her life was ruined. Yet, Horace's cheating did not stop her from being in love after all. Therefore, she could no longer avoid his calls. She gave in shortly after he stopped by, and they vowed to always be together. One month later, just after her sixteenth birthday, she discovered she was pregnant. She kept the pregnancy a secret.

Everyone began noticing a change in her attitude. She got into a physical fight with her aunt on two separate occasions. The first fight was over something very petty. Brittany's aunt told her to get off the phone, and she didn't want to. A fierce argument ensued, and the aunt pushed her out of her room. Brittany hit the aunt, and the fight went on from there. Things escalated when a knife came into play, and no one could discern what was really going on!

Brittany attempted to keep her pregnancy a big secret, but she wasn't good at hiding things. Hence, she got up the nerve to tell her mother about the pregnancy. Needless to say, her mother was destroyed and couldn't understand how her sixteen-year-old daughter could make such a poor decision. She reminded her daughter that they were struggling, and barely had a place to stay. But Brittany wasn't trying to hear any of her mother's pleas; she was pregnant, and that was all that mattered to her. After her confession, she wanted everyone to know about her pregnancy, and I think she thought it was cute. This girl talked about being pregnant to anyone who would listen. If you dared confront her about it being a mistake, she would say, "You are just jealous!"

The pregnancy was definitely a bad decision, and everyone realized it except for Brittany. She didn't think about where she would live with her child; she only wanted to have her baby. She wanted someone to love her, and this was her golden opportunity. The pregnancy was hard for everyone else to accept, and her starry-eyed hope dwindled when Horace denied being the father. His rejection cut her so deeply she would walk around crying all day as her hormones intensified the emotional blow.

School was becoming boring, and she couldn't get up on time to make it to class. That's when she decided to attend a school for pregnant teenagers. She felt better emotionally attending a school with young girls just like her. As the months began to pass, her stomach grew bigger, and she grew out of her clothes. Brittany was now unhappy with her physical appearance and the pregnancy. Her living situation was becoming more strained, and she also noticed the look on people's faces when she brought baby items into the house. The overcrowding and bringing in another mouth to feed sparked constant arguments. Brittany's combativeness made her aunt, sister, and mother extremely unhappy. In all honesty, Brittany was mad at herself for her decision and was taking it out on everyone else. She really just wanted everyone to agree with the outcome of her present situation.

Her stream of bad decisions continued when she decided to apply for public assistance. This grant would provide her with cash and food supplements that her mother already received for the family. However, she thought it was a good idea to receive her assistance separately. Brittany knew this would reduce her mother's aid, but it didn't matter because she didn't care about everyone else.

Others repeatedly tried to tell her that it was a terrible idea to get involved in the system at such a young age, especially when she didn't need to. And they were right-Once she received her food-stamp card, she barely contributed to the household; instead, she gave it to her boyfriends' mother or loaned it to her friends. When it came to purchasing groceries for where she lived, she made excuses, and the groceries never made it home. Her aunt grew tired of her excuses, where her mother never said anything to correct the situation. It was kind of like she had given up hope of her daughter ever doing any better. Really, no one had given up hope on her; they were disgusted with her attitude and behavior.

Her relationship with Horace was always rocky, meaning they were together one day and apart the next. Horace didn't want to be around Brittany on a daily basis, and she couldn't understand that. She had high expectations for this glorious relationship now that she was pregnant. But he wasn't living up to her standards. She talked about them moving in together and even getting married, but as the pregnancy progressed, they grew further apart.

Brittany had a horrible attitude and blamed everyone for her pre-existing issues. She believed everyone was supposed to cater to her, but on the contrary, everyone was distancing themselves.

The school year ended with Brittany looking forward to having a child in just two short months. Her final grades were average, and her relationships were steadily deteriorating. Now that school was over, she started spending nights out all the time or coming home so late that everyone was asleep when she returned. She continuously disappeared, and when anyone tried to talk with her about it, she lashed out. In time people stopped showing concern and left her to her own devices.

The summer was almost over when she called her aunt and uncle to ask if she could move into their home when she had the baby. After they talked it over amongst their children, they decided that it would be wise for Brittany and her child to be in a more stable environment. When she learned that she was welcomed, she told everyone about her move. I tried to talk with her about the move because I knew the family very well and she wasn't going to be allowed to do the same things at their house. They had four sons who had curfews, chores, and followed the rules- if they didn't, there were consequences. Brittany wasn't used to rules, or maybe she didn't know how to follow them. At any rate, she decided not to heed the warnings and began moving her belongings to their home.

Two weeks after inquiring about the move, Brittany went into labor while at home. It was a Thursday night, and Horace was with her as she hollered with each excruciating contraction. Frantically, they called around, trying to find transportation to the hospital because Horace didn't have a ride or money for a cab. Neither did anyone else. At long last, they secured a ride at the height of Brittany's intense contractions. At one point she didn't know how she would make it through labor. As the night went on, she continued asking for pain medication because she could no longer bear the pressure of her uterus opening to give birth. Finally, it was time for her to push. The doctor had to take certain precautions due to warts being present at the time of delivery.

After the tenth push, the baby forcefully tore through her cervix, ultimately requiring about five stitches. She was now holding a healthy baby boy, and not long after, sheer exhaustion sent her right to sleep. Being a mother was no longer a figment of her imagination but was now a reality.

Two days after giving birth, it was time for Brittany to adjust to her new living arrangement. Her brother picked her up from the hospital, and they proceeded to her aunt's home. Her grandmother came over to assist her for the first few days at home. Brittany wasn't enjoying getting up every few hours to feed her baby. Coping with the new addition to her life was becoming frustrating for her. Three days later, the baby was due for his first doctor's appointment, so her uncle dropped her off at her grandmother's place the day before. Brittany never changed the baby's primary doctor, which caused her to travel further with little or no carfare. This made things a lot harder for her because she had burned so many people when she was pregnant with her bad attitude that nobody wanted to help her.

Being at her grandmother's place surpassed one day and turned into several days. She didn't want to go back to her uncle's house, where there was so little help, and Horace was not allowed. This made her think maybe she shouldn't have moved out, but it was too late, the deed was done.

Her six-week maternity leave was over, and it was time for Brittany to return to school. Classes where she attended school started three weeks earlier than CPS. Needless to say, she wasn't really feeling like going back to school. She was basically fending for herself when it came to the baby. But the rules were that she would go to school and take her baby with her to the on-site daycare. Their policy required her to pick the baby up exactly when school was over. This schedule demanded that she be a 24/7 single parent. These rules left her with no free time to get pregnant again.

Shortly after learning the rules, she decided to cause havoc to get back to her grandmother's house because she wanted to be free to come and go as she pleased. Brittany left her uncle's house one weekend and was supposed to be at her grandmother's home. But after her uncle called and spoke with her mother, he found out that she wasn't there, and he became furious. He called Brittany and told her that she lied about her whereabouts and that her behavior was unacceptable.

She was at Horace's house and had been there the whole weekend. The uncle let her know that this wasn't something he was willing to tolerate. So, either she would stay at his home, or she was going back to stay with her mother. This led to Brittany's usual drama with the narrative that her aunt and uncle were picking on her, and she was ready to come back home. She called her brother, who came to retrieve her things. Brittany got her mother to enroll her in the school where her cousin attended. She was behind, but once she began to participate regularly, she got the hang of things. Brittany loved being back at home with so many people and not having to come right home after school. Moreover, she didn't have to attend to her child if she didn't want to.

To make matters worse, she was coming home at nine or ten on a school day as if it were normal. Her excuses were worse than her behavior. She would say that her teacher gave her finals after school or the bus broke down. Worst of all, her mother never said a word to her about her actions. Not addressing the issue made Brittany more of a liar about her whereabouts. Whenever she arrived home, she would always have a sad story about being tired and that someone should watch her baby while she eats and does her homework. However, her exhaustion never stopped her from talking on the phone until the wee hours of the morning. Which made her late for school almost every day.

Still, her mother never said a word, just walked around in silence evading her daughter's troublesome issues. Not having any accountability allowed Brittany to heap more grief onto her mother by blaming her for everything in her life. Instead of thanking her, she told her mother that she ruined her life by not advising her that being a mother was hard.

Brittany's mother was noticeably weary from fighting her own battles. She loved her daughter, but going through a divorce, didn't leave her much energy to support her. Brittany used the guilt her mother felt to get away with murder. After the baby's birth, her mother basically gave up hope for her daughter and felt like she was too far gone to be willed back to reality.

In the wake of such situations, I continue to tell people you can't allow your children to walk all over you. Most importantly, you can't give up on them when they make bad decisions. My assessment of Brittany is that she was hurting and didn't know how to ask for help.

That's why it was surprising when the aunt she constantly fought began keeping the baby while Brittany attended school. Her aunt, however, wasn't going to allow her to come home whenever she felt like it, so she gave Brittany a timeframe to make it home. If she got out of school at 2:45 pm, she had until 5:00 pm to get home. For every five minutes after 5 pm that Brittany was late, there would be a one-dollar fee. So, after being chronically late several times, her aunt implemented the rule.

Brittany cried and screamed, feeling this was unfair and claiming she didn't have any money to pay the extra fees. Her aunt reminded her that in the real world and in daycare, these are the charges that will occur whether she can pay or not! If she decides not to pay, her child will no longer be allowed to return to school!

Her aunt's words fell on deaf ears because Brittany didn't change. In her absence, her mother, who worked from twelve to eight in the morning, got her son from her aunt until she arrived home. This became a regular practice, and nobody said a word.

Horace no longer dated Brittany due to her dramatic behavior and the fact that they often suspected one another of cheating. This led to their decision to go their separate ways.

Shortly after the separation, Brittany found someone else to date. This young man was older than her, but he was in school and aware of her situation. Brittany really appreciated him not judging her for having a child. To raise her confidence, he took her to meet his mother. While she felt honored, she was finding it hard to keep her mind off Horace. She tried her best not to act on impulse, and surprisingly, it worked for a while. This young man liked her so much he brought her a cell phone to keep in touch. Moreover, every weekend, she would go and spend the night with him. She was seventeen years old by this time, still breaking the rules.

What really surprised everyone was when others gave their input on Brittany's behavior, how quickly her mother jumped to her defense. Therefore, no one wanted to be around her because they knew it would lead to an argument in her favor. Yet, the young man she was dating thought that Brittany was a great person and was crazy about her son. In turn, she reassured him that Horace no longer had a place in her life. It was shortly after, that her new man gifted her with a cell phone in his name, which Brittany continuously abused by going over her minutes. Although she was paying her own bill, it made him uneasy that she would misuse the phone service and take advantage of his trust. Brittany disregarded this young man's feelings and started talking to

Horace again. As a matter of fact, the two of them laughed and played all night on the phone. Brittany's aunt advised her that her actions were unacceptable- to no avail.

Horace began to come back around, and now she was receiving attention from both young men. She found it very fulfilling to juggle two men simultaneously- as a matter of fact, she loved it! Therefore, she continued, spending alternate nights out with the two young men. No one said a word about her immorality. Living this kind of life made her feel loved, and all she wanted more than anything was for a man to love her. Now, she had two men loving her, and it made her feel larger than life. But in reality, she was deemed easy and disloyal.

Brittany juggled these young men until her boyfriend noticed a specific phone number on her phone bill printout. He confronted her about the number, and she lied at first, then panicked because she didn't want him to find out that it was Horace's number. Crying, she tried to explain herself but failed miserably. He asked why she didn't tell the truth at first, and Brittany had no explanation. He then called her a liar, a cheat, and a whore as well- This really hurt, and she responded by arguing in defense of her questionable character. In the end, she cried, but he requested the return of his phone. Afterward, he decided not to see Brittany anymore and terminated her phone service. This rendered her unable to talk to Horace all night long.

Brittany couldn't grasp that she had been caught up and dumped so ruthlessly. The breakup lowered her self-esteem, so, as a pick-me-up, she immediately began to focus on Horace. This didn't help either because they fought all the time, and Brittany would come home with bruises on her neck. But she always lied about where she had been. In the same fashion, Horace would have scratches on his face. This made me believe that the abuse was mutual.

Once Brittany's grandmother continued to see her come home with bruises, she began advising her not to put her hands on someone because she didn't like what they said or did. The same things were said to Horace. Yet, after numerous interventions, they continued to fight. Brittany was persistent when it came to seeing Horace, and no one could stop her.

When Brittany's child turned eight months old, she began looking for an apartment for herself, her mother, and her siblings. Things were very intense during this time as her father had sued her mother for custody of the children. He even requested child and spousal support. Everyone knew his claim was ludicrous- Brittany was unwanted by her father. Once he was granted custody, he planned on emancipating Brittany.

It took two months to find a nice apartment, but her selection put her mother under financial strain. Nevertheless, her mother complied with the rental agreement because her current situation had become unbearable. Everyone at her grandmother's home was excited for them to be leaving because it had been two years of nonstop chaos. And although her mother was excited about the move, she wasn't excited about the babysitting situation.

The moving process took about four days because Brittany's mother could not afford a U-Haul to transport their belongings. She only had clothes, a refrigerator, and a stove-other than that, she moved with no beds or furniture. Still, they were ecstatic to have their own place.

After the move, Brittany could not pick her son up on time from daycare because she was running the streets. She would rather be outside until the last minute before she returned to pick him up. The daycare was tired of her excuses, and they began to charge her. Brittany became upset because the late fees interrupted the way she planned to spend her welfare check. The daycare issue became a dilemma, one that inspired her to devise a plan- maybe a better word would be "scheme."

The scheme involved making people feel sorry for her. She began by calling around, but her first target was her grandmother. While crying, she asked if her son could stay with her for a week, and she would come every day after school and leave at night when he went to sleep. Without hesitation, Grandma told her that this was an invasion of her privacy and that the arrangement would not work. She was made to understand that being a mother was a hard job that lasted forever, and she should have listened. Brittany continued to cry and say that she really needed help, but no one would help. Grandma consoled her and got off the phone immediately when she stopped crying. She felt like everyone had turned their back on her, but in reality, she had burned her own bridges.

Her junior year had now come to an end, and her grades were reasonably good despite the circumstances. It was the summer of 09, and things were rough in the CHI, but Brittany couldn't wait to hit the streets. With her mother working nights, it wasn't long before Horace was at her home all the time as if he paid a portion of the rent. Almost every day when her mother went to work, Brittany left the house or had company over. On several occasions, her mother would come home in the morning and find evidence of people being in her home like beer bottles in the trash, cards on her dining room table, and food on the stove. Brittany's mother had no time for this foolishness or the energy to keep correcting her daughter. She was too concerned with her life to deal with anyone else's. So, her mother wouldn't say a word about these gatherings, and she just prayed for Brittany's eighteenth birthday to arrive.

Whenever her daughter wasn't throwing parties, she was sneaking out of the house, leaving the baby with whoever was at home. It didn't bother Brittany that her younger sister was just thirteen and shouldn't be at home, by herself with the baby, just as long as she could be outside. Things reached a low point when she left her child at home with her sleeping mother. This was extremely stressful for her mom, who worked the night shift and spent her mornings trying to find Brittany.

Sadly, she never answered her mother's calls; she simply strolled in when she felt like coming home. In addition to her horrible behavior, she'd found herself a new male friend with whom she argued all the time. Sometimes their arguments escalated to a point where the police were called! It was shameful that Brittany hadn't been in the new neighborhood for three months, yet everyone knew her, especially all the guys. By no means was this new environment helping her become a better woman or mother. She just couldn't seem to get her act or attitude together. She thought that everyone owed her something because she chose to get pregnant and have a child.

Brittany is seventeen now, still living life in the fast lane while struggling to raise a child alone. I don't know if she will ever change, although it's never too late to turn things around. A good place to start would be respecting and appreciating those people who have her best interest at heart. She has her whole life ahead of her, and although she has a lot to learn, I wish her the absolute best.

**RACE
RIOT
JESSE**

I've known Jesse since my sophomore year in high school. She is light skinned with big round eyes and slightly curvy. I found her to be a cool girl who I learned to love, as such she became one of my dearest friends. In time, I found out that she had a gorgeous three-year-old child. Everyone in school knew about the baby as well, and openly gave her the side-eye about her situation. However, I wasn't bothered by her having a child and got to know her better because she was a good-hearted person- that was all that mattered to me.

Jesse's child was born in July of 1997, shortly after she graduated from eighth grade. Meaning she was pregnant her entire eighth-grade year. Needless to say, this made her life exceedingly difficult. Imagine a thirteen-year-old being pregnant at such a time! It had to be hard. Come to find out, she lost her virginity immediately after her thirteenth birthday. During this time, she was completely immersed in a young man named Tony. He was a year older than her, and they basically grew up together.

Tony was a handsome young man who dressed nice and lived at home with his mother and two sisters. He had jet black hair with a caramel complexion and grew up fast in a rough neighborhood. This allowed him to mimic the older guy's behavior. Despite his mentality, Jesse admired Tony's personality and began to like him even more. Soon after they started dating, Jesse lost her virginity. She explained her first sexual experience as painful yet pleasurable. According to her, Tony was very experienced sexually eased the pain with his foreplay. Now I know you're thinking how on earth a fourteen-year-old knows about foreplay, but it was apparent that it wasn't his first time.

Although she enjoyed her sexual experience with him, she felt guilty for sneaking him into the house while her mother was away at work. It was just that having sex became a routine for them, and they were so much in love with one another. Furthermore, Jesse knew that her behavior wasn't childlike, but her curiosity overruled her conscience.

While she and Tony were in the relationship, Jesse continued to question her mother about sex. Still, her questions went unanswered, and on several occasions, she was flat out ignored. Truth be told, Jesse's mother could not provide her with the proper attention because of her work and addiction to crack cocaine. Yet, even though her mother had a drug problem, she had not allowed Jesse to go without clothes, food, or a roof over her head, ever. Her mother even made sure her hair and nails were done every two weeks. Yet, Jesse still wanted more than just things; she wanted her mother to educate her regarding her sexual feelings.

Her mother's refusal to discuss this matter led her to experiment with her sexual urges. The outcome was engaging in sexual intercourse before the age of thirteen with Tony. Perhaps, six months into their sexual relationship, Jesse had a life-altering issue- She became pregnant but didn't know right away. After a while, she could feel something moving in her tummy. This frightened her, and she was scared to tell anyone, so she kept the pregnancy a secret. A few months later, she persuaded her mother to take her to the doctor for a physical required to enter high school. As soon as the doctor examined her, he confirmed her pregnancy and asked Jesse for permission to tell her mother. Jesse nodded yes, and her mother was invited into the room. As the doctor opened his mouth, Jesse could feel cold fear, like steel, grip her entire body. She watched disappointment come over her mother's face, and not long after, they both started to cry.

Although they had a long road ahead of them, this was just the beginning. In a very palpable sense, Jesse's mother wasn't pleased with her daughter's actions. Still, she was never given the option to abort or give the child up for adoption. She only hoped her daughter understood that having a baby at her age would require much time and patience. Jesse knew that no words could describe what her mother was feeling at the time, even though she felt a sense of relief.

As soon as they got home, Jesse's mother made a call to Tony's mother. With a trembling voice, Jesse took the phone and began disclosing the news. His mother was upset and wondered what her son was thinking to have gotten Jesse pregnant! He was already incarcerated because of his bad behavior, and now, he was going to be a father.

After she calmed down, Tony's mother expressed her feelings of concern and let Jesse know the hard struggles she had ahead of her. Tony's mom was a teenage mother also and was far from judgmental. She vowed to always be there to support them along their journey to parenthood. Jesse also called her father to give him the news. Although her parents weren't together, her father was very much involved in her life. Again, Jesse sucked up her emotion and spoke with a trembling voice when delivering the devastating news. Her father had very few words to say to his little girl as she had grown up much faster than he anticipated. Their conversations then became scarce as she had disappointed him for not being careful with her life and future.

The after-effect of everyone's reaction to the pregnancy was harsh. Especially from the older people who knew she was about to be a parent. They looked at her differently, not as the same young lady they once knew. Moreover, they couldn't gather where the sexual nature had come from. The whole thing seemed an oddity that drew rude remarks from people when she passed by. Nevertheless, their reactions didn't really affect how she felt about herself. She continued to walk with her head high and never regretted having sex at the age of twelve.

The months continued to pass, bringing Jesse's school year and pregnancy to an end. Tony had come home right before her graduation, and they spoke about the pregnancy. He assured her that things would work for the better. That being understood, they continued to see one another, but Tony would not stop seeing other girls as well. This was a major concern for Jesse, who refused to allow the rumors to affect how she felt about him.

A few weeks after wobbling across the stage at graduation, Jesse went into labor which lasted for about 8 hours. She cried and wished her mother could take away the pain. Unfortunately, Tony was in summer school and was unable to make it to the hospital. Jesse's contractions were becoming more strenuous, but she never opted to take drugs. As crazy as it sounds, she probably wanted to feel all the joy and pain of her labor. Finally, it was time for her to push and, with her mother by her side, she pushed repeatedly until the baby came out. At this point, she began to gasp for air, hoping the pain was over. Finally, she heard the cry of a beautiful baby girl.

Jesse was very excited but also exhausted by the time she held her daughter. Staring in amazement at what she had just accomplished filled her with love for her daughter and she wanted to protect her with all her might. Jesse was also glad the wait was over, but two days after leaving the hospital, she didn't realize the struggle had just begun. Jesse was always at home with her daughter while her mother would go and return from work. Tony came by to help her with the baby but getting up at night and learning a whole new routine was frustrating. She was still a kid and being a mother at thirteen was a hard adjustment, but she did the best she could.

The balance of being a new high school student and a mother was new to her- It wasn't what she expected, but for the first semester, she tried hard. Regardless of her efforts, Jesse started failing and ditching her classes every time she got a chance. Her daughter was at home with her mother, and Jesse took her time getting home. School just wasn't something she took seriously, and for a while, there were many distractions in her life. The biggest one of all was her relationship with Tony; one minute, they were working things out, and the next, they were not speaking to one another. Some girl even approached her about her and Tony's involvement. That's how she found out that he was having a secret relationship with a girl from the neighborhood.

Tony had moved on, and Jesse was disturbed by the news. When she confronted him with the hearsay, he bluntly admitted that he was seeing someone else. As bad as she felt, she knew Tony was only being honest. Her pride was hurt, yet she held her head high and continued to be with him despite his relationship with other girls. By the time her freshman year was over, Jesse had failed several classes trying to manage her social life and be a parent- By the time her daughter was turning one, Jesse's life was heading downhill fast. However, this didn't stop Jesse and Tony from having sexual intercourse.

One fateful summer day, Jesse was sitting on her front porch when a girl jumped out of a car, addressing her as "Tony's Baby Momma!" This caught her off guard- She knew it was Tony's strange girlfriend because she had been threatening her the whole summer. Now she was approaching her with several other young ladies exchanging hurtful words. One girl among them called Jesse out, and Jesse hauled off and hit her in the face. They proceeded to jump her, not realizing that her friends were close by-about five of them. Immediately they came retaliating on behalf of their friend. They all fought for what seemed like hours but was actually a couple of minutes. They rumbled in the middle of the street until people on the block came to intervene. Jesse and her friends fought successfully and felt victorious. This gave her the confidence that they would no longer threaten her. For some time, this made her feel great.

The summer was almost over, and the resumption of class was near. Jesse was well pleased with her mother's decision to keep her daughter while she attended school. She would get up in the morning at 6:00am, feed her daughter, and get ready for school. By 6:45am, she had vacated the house to get on the bus to school. Jesse went to school not knowing what to expect from her fellow classmates. She was really afraid to meet new people because she didn't want to be judged and couldn't take any more criticism.

After school became a routine, Jesse became more popular, learning that she wasn't the only young lady who had a baby at such a young age. She became very fond of a teacher who just had a baby also-her name was Ms. Levens. Jesse always looked forward to Ms. Levens' class because she felt comfortable there and received advice about her child and troubles. Due to Jesse having double period English, she only had Ms. Levens for half of the school year. When she couldn't speak with Ms. Levens on a daily basis, Jesse lost focus and began to withdraw from school.

As the year progressed, she became more and more distracted. She was hanging around girls who only came to school to meet up and hang out with the guys. Learning was never their primary objective. Pretty soon, Jesse and her cohorts were smoking marijuana, and on some occasions, they added drinking. Once the party was over, Jesse would put on her book bag and return home to her child. Although she was failing, Jesse was having the time of her life in high school. Only now, instead of feeling like she could make a change, she allowed people to change her. She was simply becoming a statistic instead of fighting the odds.

Before her freshman year was over, she had failed many classes. Seeing how far she had fallen caused her to be distraught and disappointed in herself for the first time. She tried her best to hide her grades, but with all her absences and failures, her parents had to be notified. Needless to say, Jesse's mother was not happy to hear this, and she could see the hurt in her eyes. However, her mother's disappointment and corrective measures were not enough to stop her from misbehaving. Jesse was done with the lectures and was ready to start the summer off with a bang. She couldn't wait to hit the streets and attend parties. She wasted no time getting her hair done and buying new shoes and a fresh outfit for every big summer occasion.

For those who don't know, summertime in Chicago has a way of enticing everyone outside. People wait the whole year for the weather to break so they can hang out on the block, and Jesse was no exception. This particular summer, hanging out while pushing her daughter in a stroller was what every teen mom seemed to be doing, and Jesse fit right in with the trend. Besides, she appeared older than she actually was, which made men stop and blow their car horns at her and the crew. They loved it! As a matter of fact, she had met someone who she liked very much. The only issue was that they lived on the same block where she hung out, and her child's father wasn't having it. They already spent countless days arguing over who and what she was doing and why. Yet, he couldn't explain what he was doing or why.

Jesse continued to argue with Tony while seeing her new friend on the side. She knew that Tony was seeing other girls, and it hurt her, but she decided that it was best to try and move on. Few girls could say that they loved their life and wouldn't ask for anything to be different- but she could.

Junior year arrived, and she was still short of the credits needed to graduate. Without question, Jesse had a full plate with school and working a job to take care of her daughter. Life was becoming nothing but work for her, and she knew it was only going to get more challenging when trying to make up the credits she needed. She cried several mornings when getting ready for school because she was exhausted and felt she couldn't keep going. Thankfully, her friends made an effort to encourage and give her the strength to continue on.

Her social life no longer existed; thus, she missed basketball games, dances, and pep rallies because she didn't have the time. Yet, her grades were progressing, and this helped her feel better about the hard work she was putting in. Halfway through her junior year, she met a young man who attended school with us. Though she didn't like him initially, the pressure, he applied caused her to give in to him. We never thought the relationship would go far, but it surprised us all.

This guy's name was Ricky- he was kind of chubby, very light-skinned, and average looking. I personally didn't care for him because I thought he was too immature for Jesse's situation. He was the kind of guy that allowed his friends to dictate his relationships. In this particular situation, they felt that Jesse being a teen mother made her too advanced. Whenever Ricky was alone with his friends, they would not stop making fun of him regarding Jesse's past.

Personally, I never believed he had intentions of a long-term relationship with Jesse, but after they dated for some months, things began to get serious between them. Shockingly, Jesse really liked Ricky because he wasn't the average boy she would date. She usually wanted guys that were thuggish (or better yet, the "bad boy" type). Ricky was what we referred to as being a lame, yet she loved him. Their love grew, and everyone was surprised at Jesse's new era of contentment-mk. She smiled and remained cool all the time; finding love was helping her become a better person. She felt the love that she had longed for since she broke up with her daughter's father.

Gradually she started coming to class and participating. Likewise, her new crowd was focused on graduating as well. This was all well and good, but I never liked Ricky because he seemed like someone trying to use Jesse to satisfy his sexual desire. I kept this thought to myself because he treated her well and spent lots of time with her and her daughter. It looked as if things were going great between them until we graduated. Who would have thought that after having so much fun together, there would be a bump in the road of their sweet relationship?

Right before everyone was getting ready to graduate, Ricky's attitude changed towards Jesse, and he became real flaky. Several times, she questioned him, but he wouldn't give her a definite answer. She wondered why he wasn't coming over to her house or inviting her over to his, and she became upset. At this time, she wasn't talking to or entertaining other guys as the thought hadn't crossed her mind.

The day came when the whole senior class was on their way to Florida. While they were gone, we all hung out at the mall and held down jobs. Apparently, this was nothing compared to what was going on in the most magical place on earth. Jesse became concerned because she hadn't received a call from Ricky. Deep down inside, I think she knew something suspicious was going on in Florida, and it was only a matter of time before we all knew the truth.

Spring break was over, and it was time for our final exams. The grade we received would determine if we graduated. Not long after, Jesse was in the lunchroom when it was rumored that Ricky had a great time with a girl named Tiara while in Florida. Tiara knew about Jesse and Ricky's relationship. Still, despite her knowledge, Tiara would always be in Ricky's room every night naked. At the time, it was undetermined if they had sex. However, Jesse was distraught and didn't understand why he would act in such a deceitful way.

Over time, she confronted him, but he repeatedly denied it. He promised and pleaded with her that the rumors were untrue. She believed him for a minute and tried to get all the drama behind her. She was a fighter, and at any time, if she wanted, Tiara would have gotten it, but she was trying to change her life and be calm. She knew she had given Ricky the upgrade that he so desperately needed.

It was time for prom, and Jesse was so excited and couldn't wait to put on her dress. Over the years, I have watched most of my friends suffer from missing what should be memorable moments of their childhood/teenage years, but not this time. Jesse looked elegant for prom, and everyone attested to that fact. We all enjoyed the event and the after-prom activities as well. Then a week later, there was graduation, and Jesse was unable to attend. This was sad because, although she worked hard to get better grades, it didn't pay off in time. She even went to night school to make up for classes and still fell short of graduating with her classmates.

Jesse had really messed up her sophomore year by avoiding classes unnecessarily. She would leave school early to hang out with friends. Owing to that, Jesse avoided me during graduation day because she was ashamed and very disappointed in herself. However, she didn't stop there; she took the bull by the horns and went to a city college program that would allow her to get a high school diploma. She also held down a job with the determination to graduate while still dating Ricky. Our friendship was still a bit strained because she was discouraged. Still, we talked over the phone all the time and spoke a lot about Ricky's unusual behavior.

By this time, Ricky was becoming totally disrespectful, and Jesse was not happy about it. He was kind of cocky and treated her as if she was no longer necessary to him. At long last, he broke up with her, and she called to inform me about it. I asked her what went wrong and found she was emotionally derailed because Ricky had not been honest. She later found out that Ricky was dating this girl, and he dated her because she was a virgin, unlike Jesse. Ricky bragged and told everyone that he was with his new girlfriend because she was a virgin. I questioned how on earth he knew this girl was a virgin if he wasn't experienced?

It wasn't long before Jesse bounced back and was hired as a full-time worker. This led to her moving out on her own and still helping her mother pay bills. Jesse finally had her independence and a new boyfriend named Clyde. They met at work and hit the ground running. He was much older than we were by about fifteen years, dark-skinned, with a medium build. However, he was nice and seemed to help Jesse when she needed him most. Clyde lived in an apartment and was addicted to playing the lottery. Many people wondered why Jesse dated this older gentleman but what people didn't realize was that Jesse had lived a disappointing life from an early age. Now she was determined to be with someone she would enjoy the rest of her life with. Her determination helped her to accomplish her dream of graduating from high school in January 2002.

After graduation, Jesse enrolled in a food sanitation class at the school she graduated from. The license she received helped her further her career in her chosen field. Thanks to Jesse's mother, grandmother, and child's father's family, she received all the support she needed to succeed.

Statistically teenage pregancy has seen a decline yet, with all of the options the decline has not been significant. According to experts, "Thirty percent of all teenage girls who drop out of school cite pregnancy and parenthood as key reasons with only 40 percent of teen mothers finishing high school" (Shehan, 2022). With the overturning of Roe vs Wade the fight for choice has taken a major blow.

We are not allowing women or girls the right to make a choice over their lives which could be potentially harmful. This landmark case isn't only about abortion it also limits the ability to have access to birth control. Latifi (2022) stated that, "with a Roe-less future almost certainly ahead, many young people are scrambling to change their birth control methods; some are doing so to better prevent an unplanned pregnancy, while others fear birth control access could be threatened amid an assault on reproductive rights". As we address these aspects lets not forget about those who have children that are unwanted.

This life changing ruling can have an immediate affect on society. New restrictions on abortion could increase child poverty and hurt women's educational prospects, among other potential impacts on American schools (Blake, 2022). A study conducted at the University of California, San Francisco, known as "The Turnaway Study," showed people who were denied an abortion and went on to give birth experienced an increase in household poverty lasting at least four years relative to those who received an abortion. For many the right to choose can be life or death.

STATISTICS

Birth Rates for Females Aged 15 to 19 Years, by Race and Hispanic Origin of Mother: United States, 2018 and 2019

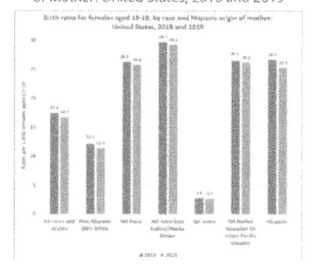

Statistics

* 64% of abortions performed on teenage women are dangerous.
* Prevalence of teenage pregnancy is higher in poor countries—95% of teenage pregnancies happen in less developed countries.
* Every year, 7.3 million teenagers around the world give birth to their first child.
* Facts about teenage pregnancy imply that teen mothers have higher chances of post partum depression, PTSD, and suicidal tendencies.
* Adolescent pregnancy statistics suggest that complications are the leading cause of both maternal and fetal deaths.
* Children born to teen mothers have higher chances of being underachievers.
* Teenage pregnancy statistics by state suggest that Arkansas and Mississippi have the highest teenage parenthood rates.

References

Blake A (2022). Overturn of Roe V Wade Coult Add to Child Proverts. Retrieved from: https://www.tc.columbia.edu/articles/2022/june/overturn-of-roe-v-wade-could-add-to-child-poverty/

CDC (2022). About Teen Pregnacy. Retrieved from: https://www.cdc.gov/teenpregnancy/about/index.htm

Latifi C (2022). Teen Vogue. Retrieved from: https://www.teenvogue.com/story/young-people-are-switching-their-birth-control-roe-v-wade

Shehan L. (2022). How Roe v Wade changed the Lives of American Women
https://www.counterpunch.org/2022/05/04/how-roe-v-wade-changed-the-lives-of-american-women/

Made in United States
Orlando, FL
17 December 2022